GERMAN

Just for Business

Irene Malcolm and Marilyn Farr

Study Guide

Oxford University Press

GW00716579

Oxford University Press Walton Street Oxford OX2 6DP

Oxford New York Toronto
Delhi Bombay Calcutta Madras Karachi
Petaling Jaya Singapore Hong Kong Tokyo
Nairobi Dar es Salaam Cape Town
Melbourne Auckland

and associated companies in

Berlin Ibadan

Oxford is a trade mark of Oxford University Press

ISBN 0 19 912144 3

Illustrations by Patricia Moffett, Joan Corlass and Gecko Limited

Acknowledgements
The authors wish to thank the following for their help in developing this course: Herr Franck (Junior), Ladage and Oelke, Hamburg; Herr Butz, Franz Glogner and Co, Norderstadt; Angela Felix, Christa Riolo and Ulrike Menzer-Black.

The Authors
Irene Malcolm is former Director of the Hants/Surrey Language for Export (LX) Centre.
Marilyn Farr is Senior Lecturer in German at Oxford Polytechnic.

Series Editors
Jane Miller and Marilyn Farr.

Printed in Great Britain by
Butler & Tanner Ltd, Frome and London

Contents

About the course

Welcome to **German *Just for Business*,** a short, practical language course for the hard-pressed business learner. This course will not turn you into a fluent German speaker overnight but it will equip you with some basic communication skills in German, and above all it will demonstrate that you are making the effort to learn the language of the country you want to do business in! It is suitable for both beginners and those with some limited knowledge of German who need a revision course with a business emphasis.

You can do most of your learning from the cassettes alone. This is because one of the aims of the course is to train you to understand spoken German on the telephone, in meetings and in other situations where you are not able to refer to the printed word. We therefore recommend that you listen to each Unit at least once before you refer to any of the printed material, apart from the *Pen and paper exercises*, in the *Study Guide*.

You'll hear a series of conversations in German, as you follow the progress of representatives of two British companies selling their products in Germany. English narrators guide you through step by step, explaining the language you hear and inviting you to join in the dialogues. The accompanying *Study Guide* contains much useful back-up information, and we strongly recommend that you use it regularly to consolidate your learning.

To get the most out of your course we recommend that you tackle it in the following way:

1 Do your initial learning of each Unit somewhere where you can really concentrate. Car journeys, though ideal for reinforcement, are not really suitable for the learning of new material.

2 Listen to the cassette as often as you can, every day if possible. 'Little and often' is the key to successful language learning. Don't expect to master a Unit by listening to it once only. You will need to listen to it several times and to replay difficult sections as often as necessary. Use pause and replay buttons if you have them and remember to make a note of the number on your tape counter as you begin a new Unit.

3 Read through the notes provided in the *Study Guide* after listening to each Unit. These notes are intended to provide you with a summary of the new language contained in each Unit and with visual reinforcement of what you have learned from the cassettes.

The notes on each Unit have five sections:

1 Language for you to use

This is the language you will need to produce yourself and therefore you should concentrate on learning and practising the language in this section. Do not go on to the next Unit until you feel you have mastered these words and expressions. Try to get someone else to test you once you have learned them thoroughly.

2 Language for you to recognize

The language in this section is what you have heard other people use on the cassette and what you must therefore learn to recognize. Although at this stage you only need a 'passive' knowledge of this language, it is important not to neglect this section as you need to understand in order to respond effectively. You may also want to 'activate' this language later on, if, for example, you are receiving instead of making a telephone call. If you already know some German, you may, of course, feel able to do this from the start.

3 Pen and paper exercises

Every now and then, if you are listening to the cassettes, you will come across the mention of a *Pen and paper exercise*. These are optional exercises which will improve your listening skills. They do not require you to write anything in German; in fact, all you usually need to do is tick a box or draw a line as you listen to the relevant part of your cassette again. Do these exercises the first time you listen to the tape if you feel ready, but some are more difficult and you may need to come back to them later.

4 Language maps

These are a summary in diagrammatic or illustrated form of the dialogues you have heard on the cassettes complete with possible variations. They will help you make up and practise your own dialogues.

5 Language debrief

As well as a brief *Language reference section* at the back, we also guide you through some basic points about the structure of the language as they come up in each Unit.

At the end of the Guide you will find a *Language reference section*, a *Vocabulary section*, the answers to the *Pen and paper exercises* and some useful tips about doing business in Germany. We also suggest how you can develop your German once you have completed this course.

Your pack also contains some prompt cards with key phrases for you to remember. You can slip them into your diary and use them for instant recall, when you are conversing in German.

Unit 1 *Making contact by telephone*

Checklist

By the end of this Unit you should be able to:

❏ get through to the right person

❏ deal with some difficulties

❏ understand when to call back.

But you'll have to wait till the next Unit to learn how to leave a message yourself!

Key words and phrases
for you to use

Greetings and introductions

Guten Tag!	*Hello, good afternoon*
Guten Morgen!	*Hello, good morning*
Auf Wiederhören	*Goodbye (telephone)*
Auf Wiedersehen	*Goodbye (in person)*
Hier spricht ...... von der Firma ...... in Southampton, England	*This is ...... from (company) ......, in Southampton, England*
Mein Name ist ...	*My name is ...*

Getting through to the right person

Ich möchte bitte Herrn Roberts sprechen	*I'd like to speak to Mr Roberts, please*
Könnte ich bitte Herrn Kunze sprechen?	*Could I please speak to Mr Kunze?*

Getting through to the right department

Die Produktionsabteilung, bitte	*The Production Department, please*

	Marketing-Abteilung	*Marketing*	
	Exportabteilung	*Export*	
Die	Einkaufsabteilung	*Purchasing*	*Department*
	Verkaufsabteilung	*Sales*	
	Rechnungsabteilung	*Accounts*	
	EDV-Abteilung	*Computer*	

Saying when you'll call back

Nein danke, ich rufe...	*No thank you, I'll call back...*
später	*later*
etwas später	*a bit later*
heute nachmittag	*this afternoon*
morgen vormittag/nachmittag	*tomorrow morning/afternoon*
übermorgen	*the day after tomorrow*
nächste Woche	*next week*
...zurück	
am Montag	*on Monday*
Dienstag	*Tuesday*
Mittwoch	*Wednesday*
Donnerstag	*Thursday*
Freitag	*Friday*
Samstag/Sonnabend	*Saturday*
Sonntag	*Sunday*
Wann könnte ich zurückrufen?	*When could I call back?*
Wann könnte ich Herrn ....../ Frau ...... erreichen?	*When could I reach Mr....../ Mrs ......?*

Other useful phrases

Guten Tag, sprechen Sie Englisch?	*Hello, do you speak English?*
Ja, natürlich/Nein, gar nicht	*Yes, of course/No, not at all*
Entschuldigung, ich verstehe nicht	*I beg your pardon, I don't understand*
Wie bitte? Wiederholen Sie das bitte!	*I'm sorry, can you repeat that please?*
Ist gut!	*Fine!*

Key words and phrases
for you to recognize

Greetings you will hear

Firma Kleist, guten Tag!	*Hello, Kleist*
Firma Herti, guten Morgen!	*Good morning, Herti*
Wie kann ich Ihnen helfen?	*How may I help you?*

Putting you through

Wer ist am Apparat?	*Who's calling?*
Bleiben Sie am Apparat!	*Hold the line*
Moment, bitte	*One moment, please* or *Hold the line, please*
Der Anschluß ist besetzt	*The line's engaged*
Wollen Sie warten?	*Do you want to hold?*
Ich verbinde Sie	*I'm putting you through*
Das Büro von Frau Backmann	*Mrs Backmann's office*
Helga Backmann am Apparat	*Mrs Backmann speaking*

Sorry, I didn't catch that

Wie bitte, wie ist Ihr Name?	*What's your name, please?*
Wiederholen Sie Ihren Namen bitte	*Repeat your name, please*
Buchstabieren Sie Ihren Namen bitte	*Spell your name, please*
Wie schreibt man das?	*How do you spell that?*

Understanding why they're not there

Es tut mir leid	*I'm sorry*
Herr/Frau ...... ist im Moment nicht da	*Mr/Mrs ...... isn't here at the moment*
Frau ...... ist heute nicht im Hause	*Mrs ...... isn't in the office today*
Er/Sie hat eine Besprechung	*He/She is in a meeting (less formal)*
Er/Sie ist ...	*He/She is ...*
in einer Konferenz	*in a meeting (more formal)*
mit einem Kunden	*with a customer*
auf Geschäftsreise	*on a business trip*
auf Urlaub	*on holiday*
krank	*ill*
beschäftigt	*busy*

And when you can call back

Sie könnten ...	*You could call back ...*
um 14 Uhr	*at 2 pm*
morgen vormittag	*tomorrow morning*
vor 11 Uhr	*before 11 o'clock*
... zurückrufen	

11

Section 3 *Pen and paper exercises*

The answers to all *Pen and paper exercises* can be found in the Section beginning on p81.

1 Listen to the tape and match the people to the departments in which they work.

1 Accounts Department   a Herr Neumann
2 Computer Department   b Herr Koppel
3 Purchasing Department   c Frau Schmidt
4 Marketing Department   d Frau Evers

2 Write down the names of people and places as the caller spells them for you.

1 _____

2 _____

3 The pictures below show the *real* reasons why the person you are calling can't speak to you. Listen to the tape and tick the appropriate box to indicate whether the reason you hear is true or false.

   True   *False*   *True*   *False*

   True   *False*   *True*   *False*

4 Listen to Herr Henschel's secretary and enter in your diary
below when you and Herr Henschel are both free to talk to each
other on the phone.

Sunday

Monday   *11.00 – 12.00 Meeting*
          I. Johnson, Braun u.k.
          TODAY

Tuesday   *– Keep free –*

Wednesday   *Presentation to*
          Franco British Chamber,
          Le Havre – All day.

Thursday *3.30 Dep. Heathrow –*
          Madrid BA 428.

Friday   *Dep. Madrid 7.30 pm.*

Saturday

Language debrief

Saying what you would like to do

Ich möchte ...	*I'd like to ...*

In order to say that you would like to do something, start the phrase with **ich möchte** and add the verb (that is the word for an action) e.g. *to speak* - **sprechen**, *to meet* - **treffen**, *to reach*, or *to get in touch with* - **erreichen** at the end of the phrase. For example:

Ich möchte Frau Scheer sprechen	*I'd like to speak to Mrs Scheer*
Ich möchte Herrn Knebel treffen	*I'd like to meet Mr Knebel*
Ich möchte Frau Sietz erreichen	*I'd like to get in touch with Frau Mrs Sietz*

To be sure of a sympathetic hearing, you should add the word **bitte**, or *please*, as in the following example:

Ich möchte **bitte** Frau Scheer sprechen

The Germans say, literally, *I would like Herrn Knebel to meet*. It may seem a bit strange at first to put the action - that is the main verb - at the end of the phrase, but you soon get used to it. Do remember that it comes right at the end:

Ich möchte Frau Scheer nächsten Montag sprechen	*I'd like to speak to Mrs Scheer next Monday*

Asking if you could...

To extend your repertoire you also have on your tape the phrase:

Könnte ich bitte ...?	*Could I please ...?*
Könnte ich bitte Frau Meier sprechen?	*Could I speak to Mrs Meier, please?*

This phrase works in exactly the same way as **Ich möchte ...** with the action coming *right at the end*.

Könnte ich Frau Meier nächsten Montag zurückrufen?	*Could I phone Mrs Meier back next Monday?*
Könnte ich bitte Herrn Wamms morgen vormittag treffen?	*Could I meet Mr Wamms tomorrow morning?*

Inviting someone to do something

Wollen Sie ...?	*Do you want to ...?*
Wollen Sie warten?	*Do you want to wait?*

This phrase works in exactly the same way as **möchte** and **könnte**.

Wollen Sie Herrn Kuhn heute nachmittag sprechen?	*Do you want to speak to Mr Kuhn this afternoon?*
Wollen Sie morgen vormittag zurückrufen?	*Do you want to phone back tomorrow morning?*

Addressing gentlemen!

Herr Jakobs becomes **Herrn** Jakobs when you want to speak to him, phone him back, see him, meet him etc. So you would always say:

Ich möchte Herrn Jakobs sprechen	*I'd like to speak to Mr Jakobs*
Ich möchte Herrn Klein erreichen	*I'd like to get in touch with Mr Klein*
Ich möchte Herrn Meier sehen	*I'd like to see Mr Meier*

Introducing yourself

In German you have to be a bit careful about how you introduce yourself. You would not say, **Mein Name ist Herr Jones,** or **Mein Name ist Frau Kelvin,** but simply: **Mein Name ist Jones.** Or you could give your full name rather than use **Herr** or **Frau.**

15

So you might say:

Jennifer Dolan am Apparat   *Jennifer Dolan speaking*

It would be rather impolite to introduce yourself as **Herr** or **Frau**. One thing that has changed in the German language in recent years is the use of **Fräulein** which is now very uncommon in the workplace. In practice, all women of 18 years and over are addressed as **Frau**.

Auf Wiedersehen *or* Auf Wiederhören?

Auf Wiedersehen, as you probably know, means *goodbye*. Its literal meaning is *until we see each other again*. **Auf Wiederhören** is used instead on the telephone and also on radio, since it means literally, *till I hear from you again*.

A word about zurück

This is a very useful word which literally means *back*, for example:

zurückrufen	*to call back*
zurückgehen	*to go back*
zurücksehen	*to look back*

What you have to remember too is that **zurück** not only means *back*, it also comes at the end of the phrase, except when it is used with **möchte, könnte** or **wollen Sie?,** as shown above. Hence:

Ich rufe Herrn Meier morgen vormittag um 11 Uhr zurück	*I'll phone Mr Meier back tomorow morning at 11 o'clock*
Wollen Sie morgen zurückrufen?	*Do you want to phone back tomorrow?*

Ich *and* Sie

For almost all actions in German, that is to say with almost all verbs, the *I*, or **ich** form will end in an **-e** and the **Sie,** or *you*, will end with **-en**.

Ich erreiche	*I get in touch with*

Sie erreichen	*You get in touch with*
Ich rufe	*I call*
Sie rufen	*You call*

Easy questions

Formulating questions in German is very simple. All that is required is for the *action* to come before the *actor*, so to speak:

Sie verstehen	*You understand*
Verstehen Sie?	*Do you understand?*
Ich könnte	*I could*
Könnte ich?	*Could I?*

Language map

*Firma Klaus Bahr,
guten Tag!*

**Guten Tag, ich möchte
bitte Herrn Buhtz
sprechen.**

*Wer ist am Apparat,
bitte?*

**Mein Name ist Carter
von der Firma
Thermoglaze, in
Southampton,
England.**

*Bleiben Sie am
Apparat. Ich verbinde.*

Guten Tag, Buhtz.

**Guten Tag. Sprechen
Sie Englisch?**

Ja, natürlich.　　　*Nein, leider nicht.*

*Der Anschluß ist
besetzt. Wollen Sie
warten?*

Ja, ist gut.　　　**Nein, danke. Ich rufe
zurück.**

Etwas später

Ich verbinde Sie.

*Guten Tag, Büro Herr
Buhtz. Trude Borm am
Apparat.*

**Guten Tag. Könnte
ich bitte Herrn Buhtz
sprechen?**

*Es tut mir leid. Er ist
heute leider nicht im
Hause.*

**Wann könnte ich
Herrn Buhtz
erreichen?**

*Morgen nachmittag,
vielleicht.*

**Vielen Dank. Ich rufe
morgen nachmittag
zurück.**

Auf Wiederhören.

Unit 2 *More about telephoning*

By the end of this Unit you should be able to:

❏ deal confidently with telephone numbers

❏ leave basic details about yourself including what you are phoning about and

❏ ask for someone to ring you back.

You will also be able to make, change and cancel appointments.

Key words and phrases
for you to use

Leaving basic details about who you are

Ich bin von der Firma	*I'm from ...... Ltd*
Die Adresse der Firma ist	*The company address is ......*
Die Telefonnummer ist	*The telephone number is ......*
Die Vorwahl ist	*The code is ......*

Saying what you are telephoning for

Es geht um ...	*It's about ...*
einen Termin	*an appointment*
eine Konferenz/eine Besprechung	*a meeting*
ein Angebot	*an offer*
einen Besuch bei Ihnen/ bei uns	*a visit to you/to us.*

Leaving a message for someone to ring you back

Könnte er/sie mich vor elf Uhr dreißig zurückrufen?	*Could s/he ring me back before 11.30 am?*
Es ist (nicht) dringend	*It's (not) urgent*

Talking about appointments

Requesting an appointment

Ich möchte einen Termin mit	*I'd like an appointment with ......*
Ich möchte einen Termin mit Frau X vereinbaren	*I'd like to arrange an appointment with Mrs X*

Fixing a date

Die erste Septemberwoche, Woche 35	*The first week in September, week 35*
Ich bin ...	*I'm free ...*
am Mittwoch	*on Wednesday*
am vierten Mai	*on 4th May*
am Nachmittag	*in the afternoon*
um 10 Uhr	*at 10 o'clock*
... frei	

Changing a date

Ich möchte das Datum der Konferenz ändern	*I'd like to change the date of the meeting*
Ich möchte die Konferenz vorverlegen	*I'd like to bring the meeting forward*
Ich möchte die Konferenz aufschieben	*I'd like to postpone the meeting*

Confirming and cancelling appointments

Ich möchte den Termin am 15. Februar bestätigen/ absagen	*I'd like to confirm/cancel the appointment on 15th February*

Key words and phrases
for you to recognize

Understanding requests for basic information

Wie ist Ihr Name?	*What is your name?*
Von welcher Firma sind Sie?	*What company are you from?*
Wie ist die Adresse der Firma?	*What is the address of the company?*
Wie ist die Telefonnummer?	*What is the telephone number?*
Wie ist die Vorwahl?	*What is the code?*
Worum geht es bitte?	*What is it about, please?*
Darf ich fragen, worum es geht?	*May I ask what it's about?*

Understanding questions about messages

Wollen Sie etwas ausrichten?	*Do you want to pass on a message?*
Kann ich etwas ausrichten?	*Can I pass on a message?*
Das geht in Ordnung	*That'll be all right*
Ist in Ordnung	*That's all right*

Understanding offers of assistance

Wie kann ich Ihnen behilflich sein?	*How can I help you?*

Understanding questions about appointments

Welches Datum paßt Ihnen?	*What date suits you?*
Welcher Tag denn? *or* An welchem Tag denn?	*Which day?* *Which day?*

Ich guck' mal eben im   *I'll just check the diary*
Kalender nach

Geht es um vierzehn Uhr?   *Is 2 pm all right?*

Other useful phrases

Wieviel Uhr ist es in   *What's the time in England/*
England/in Deutschland?   *Germany?*

Meinen Sie ...?   *Do you mean ...?*

1   If the telephone number you hear does not match the one given below, write the correct version in the space provided.

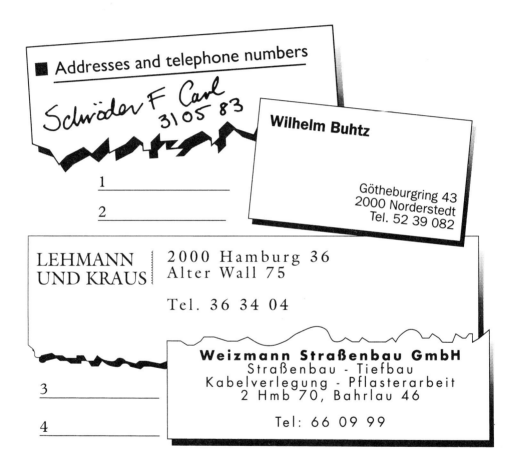

2   Say the following telephone and fax numbers aloud after you hear the question on the tape. Then listen to the correct version.

1. 54 45 08   2. 72 89 03
3. 94 15 313   4. 52 67 877

3 Listen to the three conversations on tape and draw a line to link the message number firstly with the person it is for and then with the subject of the message. Take care! We've listed more people and messages than you actually hear!

Message 1 for   a) The Director's secretary about   i) a letter

Message 2   b) The Managing Director   ii) a bill

Message 3   c) Frau Maier in Accounts   iii) a visit

                    d) Frau Müller in Sales   iv) a contract

4 Listen to the answerphone messages and complete or amend the notes as necessary.

1 Herr Eggers from Habermann called. He wants Mrs Phillips to ring him. I'm not sure what it's about, I'm afraid.

2 Urgent message from Herr Falke of Wildhusen for Mrs Cartwright, about something being cancelled. (Sorry, couldn't understand the rest!)

3 Frau Lehmann of Borgstedt rang to confirm she'll be arriving at Heathrow on Thursday at 3 pm on flight BA244.

Language debrief

Masculine, feminine and neuter

In German not just people, but all words denoting living beings, inanimate objects and concepts (nouns, grammatically speaking) have a gender, either masculine, feminine or neuter.

Other words which accompany nouns, such as the words for *the* and *a(n)*, *your*, *my* etc., or which replace nouns, such as *it* or *none*, must also take the appropriate masculine, feminine or neuter form.

Unfortunately there is no obvious logic to help one remember the gender of words. One simply has to learn them as one goes along. But don't worry about making mistakes in gender; you'll generally be understood even if you do, and most Germans do not even notice if you get a gender wrong.

'The'

Here you have to choose from **der, die** or **das** ...

der Anschluß   *the extension* is masculine

die Adresse   *the address* is feminine

das Datum   *the date* is neuter

You'll be glad to know that the plural form for *the* in all genders is **die.**

'A' and 'an'

Here again you need to learn three forms. You have come across this in Unit 2 in the phrase **Es geht um** ... - *It's about* ... In this context you have to choose from:

Es geht um **einen** Besuch   *It's about a visit* (masculine)

Es geht um **eine** Besprechung   *It's about a meeting* (feminine)

Es geht um **ein** Angebot   *It's about an offer* (neuter)

Choose the correct form of **ein** according to the gender of the noun to which it is attached. You can check this in the glossary.

Your, my, our ...

Ihr – *your*, **mein** – *my*, **unser** – *our*. These words take the same endings as **ein**. If you want to say *it's about your visit* instead of *it's about a visit*, then:

es geht um **einen** Besuch

becomes

es geht um **Ihren** Besuch (masculine)

your meeting and *your offer* would be:

Ihre Besprechung (feminine)

Ihr Angebot (neuter)

An **-e** denotes the plural. *Your meetings* is therefore:

Ihre Konferenzen (plural - all genders)

Making a date

The date is expressed in German, as in English, by means of ordinal numbers:

der erste September   *1st September*
der zehnte Mai   *10th May*

See the *Language reference section* for the formation of ordinals, as well as the names of months and days.

Making a date on ...

You will have to arrange meetings etc. *on* particular days and *on* particular dates. For this the word to remember is **am** *(on)*.

If you are arranging a date - *on the first* - then you have to use the word **am** with an -**n** added to the ordinal numbers you have above. For example:

am ersten *(on the first)*, am vierten *(on the fourth)*, am neunzehnten *(on the nineteenth)*, am zwanzigsten *(on the twentieth)*

If you are arranging your appointment on a particular day, then you simply use **am** with the day of the week. For example:

am Montag *(on Monday)*, **am** Freitag *(on Friday)*

Language map

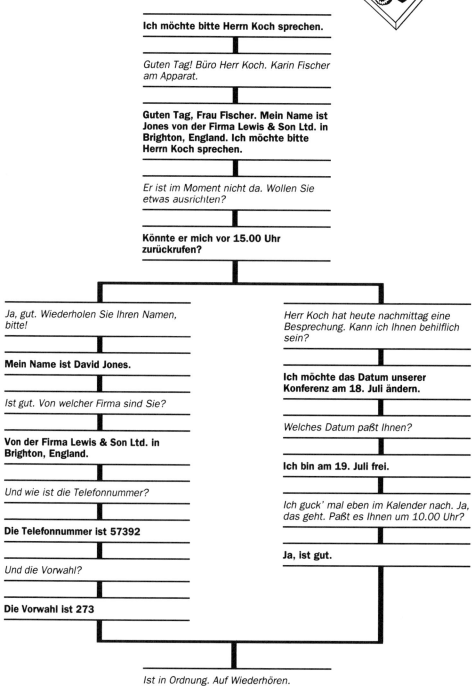

Ich möchte bitte Herrn Koch sprechen.

Guten Tag! Büro Herr Koch. Karin Fischer am Apparat.

Guten Tag, Frau Fischer. Mein Name ist Jones von der Firma Lewis & Son Ltd. in Brighton, England. Ich möchte bitte Herrn Koch sprechen.

Er ist im Moment nicht da. Wollen Sie etwas ausrichten?

Könnte er mich vor 15.00 Uhr zurückrufen?

Ja, gut. Wiederholen Sie Ihren Namen, bitte!

Mein Name ist David Jones.

Ist gut. Von welcher Firma sind Sie?

Von der Firma Lewis & Son Ltd. in Brighton, England.

Und wie ist die Telefonnummer?

Die Telefonnummer ist 57392

Und die Vorwahl?

Die Vorwahl ist 273

Herr Koch hat heute nachmittag eine Besprechung. Kann ich Ihnen behilflich sein?

Ich möchte das Datum unserer Konferenz am 18. Juli ändern.

Welches Datum paßt Ihnen?

Ich bin am 19. Juli frei.

Ich guck' mal eben im Kalender nach. Ja, das geht. Paßt es Ihnen um 10.00 Uhr?

Ja, ist gut.

Ist in Ordnung. Auf Wiederhören.

Unit 3 *Arriving at reception*

Checklist   By the end of this Unit you should be able to:

❏ announce yourself at reception

❏ say you have an appointment

❏ say what time your appointment is for

❏ introduce your colleague(s)

❏ accept/refuse refreshments politely

❏ greet your host(ess)

❏ answer a few standard questions about your health, your journey and so forth, with a few standard answers.

Key words and phrases
for you to use

At reception

Ich habe/Wir haben einen Termin mit Herrn X/ Frau Y	*I/We have an appointment with Mr X/ Mrs Y*
Ich habe einen Termin um 10 Uhr	*I've got an appointment at 10 o'clock*
Hier ist meine Karte	*Here is my card*
Eincn Kaffee? Ja bitte!	*A coffee? Yes please!*
Ja, gerne/bitte	*Yes, please*
Nein, danke	*No, thank you*
mit Zucker	*with sugar*
mit Milch	*with milk*
Ich trinke lieber Tee	*I prefer tea*

Meeting and greeting

Wie geht es Ihnen?	*How are you?*
Sehr gut, danke, und Ihnen?	*Very well, thank you, and you?*
Etwas müde? Nein, gar nicht	*A bit tired? No not at all*
Die Reise? Ganz gut, danke	*The journey? Quite good, thank you*
Darf ich Ihnen meine Kollegin/meinen Kollegen vorstellen?	*May I introduce my colleague? (female/male)*
Guten Tag, freut mich!	*Hello, pleased to meet you*

Excuses, excuses

Es tut mir leid	*I'm sorry*
Der Streik!	*The strike!*
Die Verspätung!	*The delay!*
Der Verkehr!	*The traffic!*

Responding to apologies

Das macht nichts!	*That doesn't matter!*
Das ist kein Problem!	*That's no problem!*

Key words and phrases
for you to recognize

At reception

Wie ist Ihr Name, bitte?	*Your name please?*
Kann ich Ihnen helfen?	*Can I help you?*
Um wieviel Uhr ist Ihr Termin?	*At what time is your appointment?*
Nehmen Sie bitte Platz!	*Take a seat, please*
Wollen Sie einen Augenblick warten?	*Could you wait a moment?*
Ich sage Herrn X Bescheid	*I'll tell Mr X*
Frau Y ist noch in einer Konferenz	*Mrs Y is still in a meeting*
Herr B ist noch mit einem Kunden	*Mr B is still with a customer*
Kann ich Ihnen (einen) Kaffee anbieten?	*Can I offer you (a) coffee?*
Nehmen Sie Zucker/Milch?	*Do you take sugar/milk?*
Oder trinken Sie lieber Tee?	*Or do you prefer tea?*

Meeting and greeting

Es tut mir leid	*I'm sorry*
Sie haben lange gewartet	*You've been waiting a long time*
Wie war Ihre Reise?	*How was your journey?*
Sie sind etwas müde vielleicht?	*You're a bit tired, perhaps?*
Kommen Sie bitte mit!	*Follow me, please*
Hier ist mein Büro	*Here is my office*

Pen and paper exercises

1 Listen to the two receptionists talking about the visitors they expect and complete the schedule. The visitors' names are listed below. Write the names in the appropriate spaces. Note that two visitors have an appointment at the same time.

Die Besucher: Frau Grünewald, Firma Mannesmann
Herr Schmidt, BASF
Herr Breuer, Firma Kunz
Frau Kupelwieser, Werbeagentur

Mittwoch den 26. März

Uhrzeit	Name	Termin mit
10.30		*Herr Papst* *Produktionsabteilung*
11.00		*Frau Raetz* *Marketing-Abteilung*
11.30		*Herr Dieter* *Einkaufsabteilung*
		Herr Martens *Rechnungsabteilung*

2 Can you sort out this dialogue between Liz and the receptionist? Liz speaks first.

a) *Liz:* Jim Reade und Liz Carter von der Firma Thermoglaze.

b) *Liz:* Um elf Uhr.

c) *Empfangssekretärin:* Wie ist Ihr Name, bitte?

d) *Liz:* Hier ist meine Karte.

e) *Empfangssekretärin:* Nehmen Sie bitte Platz! Ich sage Herrn
   Buhtz Bescheid.

f) *Empfangssekretärin:* Wie bitte?

g) *Liz:* Guten Tag! Wir haben einen Termin mit Herrn Buhtz.

h) *Empfangssekretärin:* Danke. Um wieviel Uhr ist Ihr Termin?

Language debrief

Verbs regular and irregular

In German there are generally three distinct forms of the verb in the present tense:

The **ich** form (I) which ends in -**e**
The **er, sie, es** form (he, she, it) which ends in -**t**
The **wir** (we), **Sie** (you) and **sie** (they) form which ends in -**en**

German verbs, like English verbs, divide into two categories, regular (in German grammar these are called *weak* verbs) and irregular (or *strong* verbs). In German, as in English, irregular verbs often have a change of letter in the middle of the word (e.g. she swims, she swam). When you look up a verb in the dictionary, it is given in its basic form, or infinitive, which ends in -**en** e.g. to meet is **treffen**, to telephone is **telefonieren.** You'll find the dictionary a useful tool, because it will tell you if the verb is irregular. Most dictionaries have a section where all the irregular verbs are listed together with an indication of what changes take place. Here is an example of a regular and an irregular verb:

Regular *(weak)*	**Irregular** *(strong)*
bestätigen *(to confirm)*	treffen *(to meet)*
ich bestätige *(I confirm)*	ich treffe *(I meet)*
er, sie, es bestätigt *(he, she, it confirms)*	er, sie, es trifft *(he, she, it meets)*
wir, Sie, sie bestätigen *(we, you, they confirm)*	wir, Sie, sie treffen *(we, you, they meet)*

Being

Not a chapter from a philosophical treatise, but a note on a very common, but very irregular verb, **sein** *(to be)*. Because it is so common you will no doubt learn it quickly, despite its irregularity. Here are some of the contexts in which we have so far met this verb. The complete list of forms is in the *Language reference* .

Ich bin ihre Sekretärin   *I'm her secretary*

Frau Braun ist auf Urlaub	*Mrs Braun is on holiday*
Frau Timms? Sie ist in einer Konferenz	*Mrs Timms? She's in a meeting*
Herr Reade und Frau Carter sind am Empfang	*Mr Reade and Mrs Carter are at the reception*

Telling people to do things

You will notice in Unit 3, that the receptionist tells Jim and Liz:

Nehmen Sie bitte Platz!	*Take a seat*

Frau Fuchs uses the same type of sentence when she invites Callum to come to her office. She says:

Kommen Sie bitte mit!	*Come with me*

Telling people to do things is very simple in German. All you have to do is put the action before the doer. You will meet this again in the last unit in the restaurant. Herr Buhtz suggests a dish to his guests by saying:

Nehmen Sie die Suppe!	*Take the soup*

And Frau Fuchs asks the waitress to bring cheese by saying:

Bringen Sie uns die Käseauswahl!	*Bring the cheese selection*

I could and I can

In Unit 2 we came across the polite form, *could*:

Könnte ich Herrn Lehmann sprechen?	*Could I speak to Mr Lehmann?*
Könnten Sie mich zurückrufen?	*Could you phone me back?*

You will also find it very useful to be able to recognize this somewhat irregular verb in the form which means *can*:

Kann ich Ihnen Kaffee anbieten?	*Can I offer you coffee?*
Können Sie das buchstabieren?	*Can you spell that?*

Können, like **möchte** and **wollen**, sends the main verb to the end of the phrase.

In Unit 3, Jim introduces Liz to Herr Buhtz by saying:

Darf ich Ihnen meine   *May I introduce my colleague?*
Kollegin vorstellen?

Ich darf also sends the main verb, or main action, to the end of the phrase.

A word about idiom

Language, like people, is a living thing and, also like people, different languages have their own particular character. It is often through the idiom of a language that its particular character is expressed. This is what makes learning a language interesting and challenging. An example of German idiom being quite different from English is the phrase:

Wie geht es Ihnen?   *How are you?*

Und Ihnen?   *And you?*

Germans say, literally, *How goes it to you?* Remember that **gehen** is also used to mean *suitable* as in:

Geht es um 14 Uhr?   *Is 2 pm all right?*

Being negative

Not an attitude we would wish to encourage, but sometimes it's necessary.

To say *not* (in other words to negate an action) you need to use **nicht.** To say *no* (before a *noun*) you need to use **kein.** The latter, as you'll remember from the last unit works like **ein** *(a)*, **Ihr** *(your)*, **mein** *(my)* and **unser** *(our)*.

Das ist kein Problem   *That's no problem*

Wir haben keine Milch   *We've no milk*

Wir haben keinen Tee   *We've no tea*

A word about danke *and* bitte

In Unit 3 we heard:

Nehmen Sie Zucker?	*Do you take sugar?*
Ja, bitte	*Yes, please*

Liz, however says:

Nein, danke	*No, thank you*

Watch out for the use of **danke** in response to an offer: it means you are refusing. So if you want to accept something make sure you say **bitte** and not **danke**.

Language map

Guten Tag!

Guten Tag!
Ich habe einen Termin mit
Herrn Buhtz.

Wie ist Ihr Name?

Mein Name ist Jim Reade von
der Firma Thermoglaze.

Um wieviel Uhr ist Ihr Termin?

Um elf Uhr.

Nehmen Sie bitte Platz!
Ich sage Herrn Buhtz Bescheid.

Es tut mir leid, Herr Buhtz ist
noch in einer Besprechung.
Kann ich Ihnen Kaffee
anbieten?

Ja, bitte.

Nehmen Sie Zucker?

Ja, bitte.

Es tut mir leid Herr Reade. Sie
haben lange gewartet.

Das macht nichts.

Wie geht es Ihnen?

Sehr gut, danke. Und Ihnen?

Auch gut. Wie war Ihre Reise?

Ganz gut, danke.

Darf ich Ihnen meine Kollegin
Frau Carter vorstellen?

Freut mich! Kommen Sie bitte
mit! Hier ist mein Büro.

Unit 4 *Presenting your company and its products I*

By the end of this Unit you will have learnt:

❏ how to present yourself, your company and your products

❏ how to talk about dimensions

❏ how to talk about delivery terms and payment.

You will also learn a few basic strategies for meetings and to ask business–related questions in German as you go round the German company.

Key words and phrases
for you to use

Presenting the company

Wir sind ein mittelgroßes Unternehmen	*We are a medium-sized company*
Wir existieren seit 50 Jahren	*We've been in business 50 years*
Wir stellen Fenster her	*We manufacture windows*
Wir produzieren x Fenster pro Monat	*We produce x windows per month*
Wir wollen nach Deutschland exportieren	*We want to export to Germany*
In den Niederlanden geht der Verkauf gut	*We are selling well in the Netherlands*
Wir spezialisieren uns auf ...	*We specialize in ...*
Wir haben ungefähr hundert Mitarbeiter	*We have approximately 100 employees*
Unser Marktanteil im Inland beträgt x%	*Our share of the home market is x%*
Unser Anteil am deutschen Markt beträgt x%	*Our share of the German market is x%*
Wir bringen ein neues Produkt auf den Markt	*We are launching a new product*
Unser Umsatz ist ...	*Our turnover is ...*

Presenting the product

Es eignet sich besonders gut für den europäischen Markt	*It is particularly well suited for the European market*
Die Qualität	***The quality***
Es ist ein hochwertiges Produkt	*It's a high-quality product*

leicht zu montieren	*easy to install*
modern	*modern*
praktisch	*practical*
beliebt	*popular*

Die Maße

The dimensions

Unser Produkt ist x Zentimeter lang	*Our product is x cm long*
breit	*wide*
hoch	*tall*
Unser Produkt hat einen Durchmesser von x Zentimetern	*Our product is x cm in diameter*
Es ist/Sie sind aus	*It's/They're made of ......*
Unser Produkt ist aus Aluminium	*Our product is made of aluminium*
Holz	*wood*
Pappe	*cardboard*
Kunststoff	*plastic, uPVC, etc.*
Glas	*glass*

Der Preis und die Lieferung

Price and Delivery

Wir produzieren auf Bestellung	*We make to order*
Darf ich Ihnen unsere Broschüre zeigen?	*May I show you our brochure?*
Hier ist eine Preisliste	*Here is a price list*
Wir haben interessante Preise	*We have attractive prices*
Es gibt einen Rabatt von x%	*There is a discount of x%*
Unsere Lieferzeit beträgt einen Monat/sechs Wochen	*Our delivery period is one month/six weeks*
Wir liefern frei Haus verzollt	*We deliver carriage and duty paid*
mehr als	*more than*
über	*over*
Wir möchten eine Banküberweisung	*We would like a bank transfer*
der Spediteur/die Spedition	*freight forwarder*

Meetings and strategies

Das ist eine interessante Frage!	*That's an interesting question*
Entschuldigung, sicherlich ein Mißverständnis	*I beg your pardon, a misunderstanding, no doubt*
Wenn ich Sie recht verstehe, ...	*If I've understood correctly, ...*
Sie wollen 2 000 Stück bestellen	*You want to order 2000 items/pieces*

Asking questions of the other company

Kaufen Sie Ihre Ersatzteile hier in Deutschland?	*Do you buy your parts here in Germany?*
Arbeiten Sie mit einem guten Spediteur?	*Do you work with a good freight forwarder?*
Arbeiten Sie mit großen Unternehmen?	*Do you work with big firms?*
Wer sind Ihre Kunden?	*Who are your customers?*
Wer ist Ihr Lieferant?	*Who is your supplier?*
Was für Verpackung verwenden Sie?	*What sort of packing do you use?*
Verwenden Sie Kunststoff?	*Do you use plastic?*

Useful phrases

Das stimmt!	*That's true!*
Das kommt darauf an	*That depends*

Key words and phrases
for you to recognize

Understanding questions about your company

Wie hoch ist Ihr Umsatz?	*What is your turnover?*
Wieviele Niederlassungen haben Sie?	*How many branches have you got?*
Wieviele Fabriken haben Sie?	*How many factories have you got?*
Wieviele Fenster/Pullover produzieren Sie ...	*How many windows/jumpers do you produce ...*
pro Woche?	*per week?*
pro Monat?	*per month?*
Wieviele Produkte umfaßt Ihr Sortiment?	*How many products are there in your product range?*

Understanding questions about your products

Welche Maße hat das Produkt?	*What are the dimensions of the product?*
Wieviele Modelle haben Sie?	*How many models have you got?*
Alle Größen?	*All sizes?*
Haben Sie ...... auf Lager?	*Have you got ...... in stock?*
Aus welchem Material ist das Produkt?	*What material is the product made of?*
Entspricht Ihr Produkt den neuen europäischen Industrienormen?	*Does your product conform to the new European standards?*
Liefern Sie Ersatzteile?	*Do you supply (spare) parts?*

Understanding questions about delivery terms and payment

Produzieren Sie auf Bestellung?	*Do you manufacture to order?*

Haben Sie eine Preisliste?	*Do you have a price list?*
Geben Sie Rabatt?	*Do you give discounts?*
Wie lang ist Ihre Lieferzeit?	*What is your delivery time?*
Wie sind Ihre Zahlungsbedingungen?	*What are your terms of payment?*
Können Sie ein Angebot in D-Mark machen?	*Can you give us a quote in German marks?*

Understanding your guide on the tour of the premises

Rechts/links haben wir ...	*To the right/left we have ...*
das Lager	*the storage area*
die Verpackungsabteilung	*the packing department*
Was für Verpackung verwenden wir?	*What sort of packaging do we use?*
Ich zeige Ihnen ...	*I'll show you ...*

1 Listen to Jim enumerating the benefits of Thermoglaze's windows and number the statements reprinted below 1-5 in the order in which you hear them. Can you find which one he has left out?

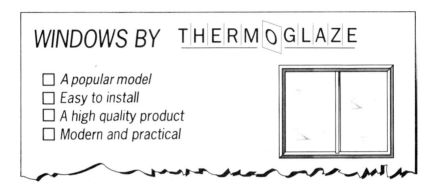

WINDOWS BY THERMOGLAZE

☐ *A popular model*
☐ *Easy to install*
☐ *A high quality product*
☐ *Modern and practical*

2 Listen to the conversations and fill in the dimensions.

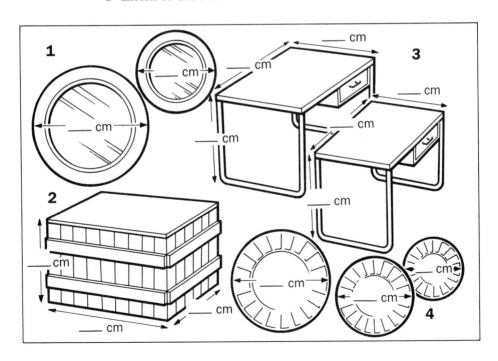

Section 4 **Language debrief**

How long did you say?

Thermoglaze has been in existence for 50 years. Liz tells Herr Buhtz:

Wir existieren **seit** fünfzig Jahren

Notice that in German we say literally *we exist* - **wir existieren**, rather than *we have existed.* In this sentence **seit** means *for*, but it is also used to mean *since* as in the following example:

Wir existieren **seit** 1950   *We've been in existence since 1950*

Asking how many (wieviele)? or how much (wieviel)?

Wieviele Fenster produzieren Sie pro Woche?	*How many windows do you make each week?*
Wieviel Plastik kaufen Sie?	*How much plastic do you buy?*

Note that here again the plural form has an **-e** at the end.

More than one

Whilst in English we mostly just add *-s* to the end of a noun to form its plural, in German there are a number of different ways of forming plurals, for example:

das Fenster/die Fenster	*the window/the windows*
die Konferenz/die Konferenzen	*the meeting/the meetings*
der Besuch/die Besuche	*the visit/the visits*

You can get help from the glossary (and indeed, from your dictionary) where all plurals are given in brackets after the noun.

He, she, it and they

As you know, even inanimate objects like windows (**das Fenster** - neuter) have a gender in German, so you will hear **er** and **sie**, as well as **es** used when referring to objects, depending on whether they're masculine, feminine or neuter.

Der Schreibtisch ist groß	*The desk is big*
Er ist groß (masculine)	***It** is big*
Das Fenster ist rund	*The window is round*
Es ist rund (neuter)	***It** is round*
Die Konferenz ist interessant	*The meeting is interesting*
Sie ist interessant (feminine)	***It** is interesting*

As in English, the German only has one plural form - *they* is always **sie**:

Die Schreibtische sind groß	*The desks are big*
Sie sind groß	***They** are big*
Die Fenster sind rund	*The windows are round*
Sie sind rund	***They** are round*
Die Konferenzen sind interessant	*The meetings are interesting*
Sie sind interessant	***They** are interesting*

'To' with countries (and most place names!)

The word which you require here is **nach.** For example:

Wir exportieren **nach** Großbritannien	*We export **to** the UK*

Nach before the name of the country is all you require for almost all countries. But two very common trading partners of the UK have plural names and are thus an exception. These are the United States and the Netherlands and here you have to say:

Wir exportieren in die USA	*We export **to** the USA*
Unsere Firma exportiert in die Niederlande	Our company exports ***to*** the **Netherlands**

What's it made of?

To say something is made of a particular material you only need to use the word **aus** *(out of)* and the material:

aus Holz	*of wood*
aus Kunststoff	*of plastic*

Talking about dimensions

There is a standard pattern you can use to express the dimensions of an object, as follows:

Er/Sie/es ist	*It's x cm ...*
x zentimeter ...	
lang	*long*
breit	*wide*
hoch	*high/tall*

Remember that with diameter it is slightly different:

Er/Sie/Es **hat** einen	*It is ...... cm in diameter*
Durchmesser **von**	
Zentimetern	

Verbs with moveable parts

In this unit you will have noticed that the verb **herstellen** fits this description and thus follows the same pattern as **zurückrufen** which you met in Unit 2:

Wir **stellen** Fenster **her**   *We manufacture windows*

If you find **herstellen** a bit awkward to use you can usually avoid it by using **produzieren** *(to produce)*.

Language map 1

Presenting your company

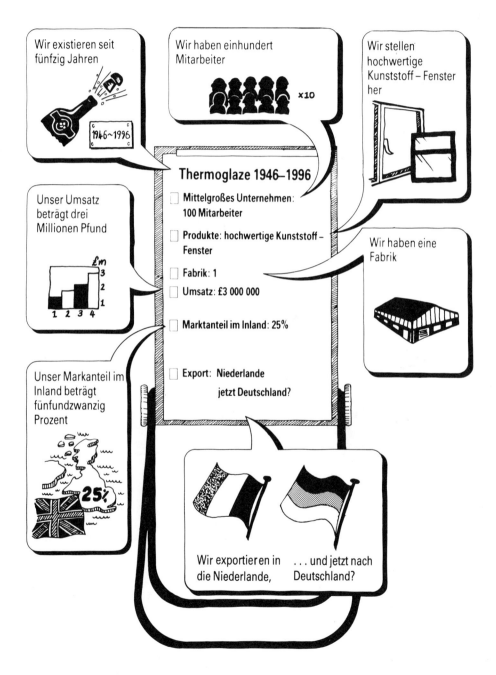

Wir existieren seit fünfzig Jahren

1946~1996

Wir haben einhundert Mitarbeiter

x10

Wir stellen hochwertige Kunststoff – Fenster her

Unser Umsatz beträgt drei Millionen Pfund

£m
3
2
1
1 2 3 4

Thermoglaze 1946–1996

☐ Mittelgroßes Unternehmen: 100 Mitarbeiter

☐ Produkte: hochwertige Kunststoff – Fenster

☐ Fabrik: 1

☐ Umsatz: £3 000 000

☐ Marktanteil im Inland: 25%

☐ Export: Niederlande
    jetzt Deutschland?

Wir haben eine Fabrik

Unser Markanteil im Inland beträgt fünfundzwanzig Prozent

25%

Wir exportieren in die Niederlande,

... und jetzt nach Deutschland?

Presenting your product

UNSER PRODUKT

ist 80 Zentimeter breit

• ist modern und praktisch

ist • aus Holz
  • aus Aluminium
  • aus Kunststoff

ist 150 Zentimeter hoch

• ist leicht zu putzen

• ist leicht zu montieren

ist ein hochwertiges Produkt

THERMOGLAZE

Language map 3

Fixing the terms

Geben Sie Rabatt?

Wie lang ist Ihre Lieferzeit?

Haben Sie eine Preisliste?

Wie sind Ihre Zahlungsbedingungen?

Ja, fünfzehn Prozent bei Bestellungen über £5000

Unsere Lieferzeit beträgt sechs Wochen

Ja, hier ist eine Preisliste

Wir möchten eine Banküberweisung

Unit 5 *Presenting your company and its products II*

Checklist In this Unit you will learn more about:

❏ presenting yourself, your company and your product.

You will also learn:

❏ how to ask and answer questions about the market

❏ how to talk in percentages.

Key words and phrases
for you to use

Introducing yourself

Ich bin Verkaufsleiter eines mittelgroßen Familienbetriebs	*I'm the Sales Director of a medium-sized family firm*

Talking about your workforce

Wir beschäftigen ... Mitarbeiter	*We employ ... workers*

Talking about your products

Wir garantieren die höchste Qualität	*We guarantee the highest quality*

Talking about your company's performance

In Deutschland ist der Verkauf dieses Jahr um 15% gestiegen	*Sales in Germany have increased by 15% this year*
In den USA und in der EG geht der Verkauf gut	*We're selling well in the USA and in the EC*

Talking about your customers

Die Deutschen verstehen etwas von Qualität	*The Germans understand quality*
wie die Amerikaner	*like the Americans*

Researching the market for your product

Wieviele Pullover verkaufen Sie ...	*How many pullovers do you sell ...*
pro/im Monat/Jahr	*per month/year*
pro Woche	*per week*
Wer ist der typische Kunde?	*Who is the typical customer?*
Welche Größen verkaufen sich gut?	*Which sizes sell well?*
Eignen sich unsere Modelle gut für den deutschen Markt?	*Are our models well suited to the German market?*

Talking about delivery terms and payment

Wir liefern frei Haus verzollt	*We deliver carriage and duty paid*
Sie bezahlen gegen Rechnung	*You pay against invoice*
Bei Bestellungen von 50 Pullovern geben wir 10% Rabatt	*We give 10% discount on orders of 50 pullovers*
Darf ich Ihnen unseren Katalog zeigen?	*May I show you our catalogue?*
Ich danke Ihnen	*Thank you*

Useful phrases

Ja, stimmt/ja richtig	*That's right*
normalerweise	*usually*
natürlich	*of course*

Key words and phrases
for you to recognize

Understanding the hype

Unsere Produkte sind sehr erfolgreich	*Our products are very successful*
in allen europäischen Ländern	*in all European countries*
Wir sind ein internationales Unternehmen mit Hauptsitz in München	*We are an international enterprise with headquarters in Munich*
Unser Umsatz ist über eine Milliarde	*Our turnover is more than a thousand million*
Wir haben x Niederlassungen im Ausland	*We have x branches abroad*
Wir haben nicht viel Konkurrenz	*We haven't got much competition*
Gehen die Geschäfte gut bei Ihnen?	*Is your business doing well?*
Geht der Verkauf gut?	*Are sales holding up?*

Understanding what the buyer says about the market

About the market

Im Winter verkaufen wir besser als im Sommer	*In winter we sell better than in summer*
unser typischer Kunde	*our typical customer*
Berufstätige mit gutem Einkommen im Alter von 25 bis 55	*working people with a good income between the ages of 25 and 55*
Welche Größen verkaufen sich gut?	*Which sizes sell well?*
die achtunddreißig und die vierzig	*the (sizes) thirty-eight and forty*

About your products

Ich mag Ihre Produkte	*I like your products*
Sie sind sehr interessant und originell ...	*They are very interesting and original*
... aber ich möchte andere Farben sehen	*But I'd like to see other colours*

Queries and requests from the buyer

Wie lang ist Ihre Lieferzeit ...	*What is your delivery time ...*
für Lagerartikel?	*for articles from stock?*
für Sonderbestellungen?	*for special orders?*
Haben Sie Muster?	*Have you got samples?*
Was kosten die Ersatzteile?	*How much are the spare parts?*
Haben Sie die Teile auf Lager?	*Have you got the parts in stock?*
Bestätigen Sie den Preis per Brief?	*Will you confirm the price by letter?*

Winding up

Ich danke Ihnen für Ihren Besuch	*Thank you for your visit*

1 Listen to the interviews and complete the company profiles.

HELGA HANSEN - Schönheitsprodukte

FOUNDED:

○ HEAD OFFICE:
MANUFACTURING PLANTS IN:

○ Nº OF EMPLOYEES (total):
TURNOVER:
CURRENT MARKET:
FUTURE PLANS:

○

SPIELWARENHERSTELLER -
Klaus Wickmann
FOUNDED:
FOREIGN BRANCHES IN:

Nº OF EMPLOYEES:
TURNOVER:

○

2 Listen to the interview with Frau Hansen and enter the appropriate percentages below.

% market share

Germany _____ %

USA _____ %

EC _____ %

The hatched area represents the increase in sales in that market. Enter the percentage increases in the appropriate area of the chart.

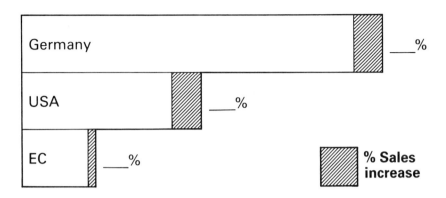

3 Listen to the conversation and complete the notes.

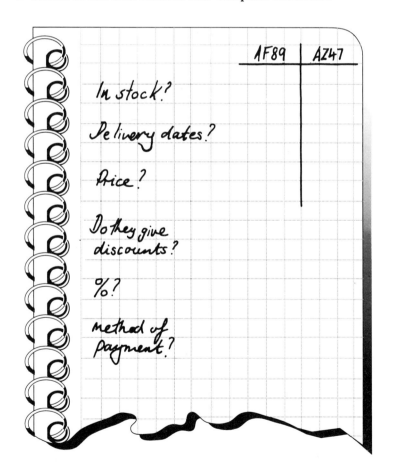

Language debrief

We specialize ourselves!

In English there are a few verbs which have to be used with an additional, or reflexive, pronoun e.g. *ourselves*, *itself* etc. Some examples of these reflexive verbs in English would be:

I wash *myself* She prides *herself*

The German equivalents are **mich** (*myself*), **sich** (*him/herself*), **uns** (*ourselves*). The German language also has many such verbs. In Unit 5, for example, Callum says:

Wir **spezialisieren uns** *We specialize in high-quality,*
auf hochwertige, *Scottish knitwear*
schottische Strickwaren

The reflexive pronoun is often not translatable into English. Liz and Jim think that their new swivel window is particularly well-suited to the European market:

Es **eignet sich** besonders *It's particularly suitable for*
gut für den europäischen *the European market*
Markt

In German one says it *suits itself* well for the European market. To form a question simply put the verb at the beginning of the sentence:

Eignen sich unsere *Are our models*
Modelle für ...? *suitable for ...?*

Watch out, however, for a change in word order if instead of naming your products, you ask *Are they suitable for ...?*:

Eignen sie **sich** für ...? *Are they suitable for ...?*

Eignet es **sich** für ...? *Is it suitable for ...?*

Here the reflexive pronoun is third and not second in the phrase.

Subject and object

To develop your ability to speak and understand the German language, you have to be able to distinguish the subject, object and verb of a sentence.

Let us look at this in a simple example. At the company reception, Jim Reade might have replied to an offer:

Ich möchte bitte einen Tee   *I would like a tea, please*

Ich is the *subject*, **möchte** is the *verb* and **einen Tee** is the *object*. Your best starting point for working out what's what in a German sentence is to find the verb, or action. Then, to find the subject, ask yourself who or what is doing the action. The next stage is to ask what or whom is the action affecting, and this gives you the object of the sentence.

See the *Language reference* section for more information about endings for subject and object.

Word order

To say in German that your market share is 9% is simply:

Unser Marktanteil ist 9%

In this sentence **unser Marktanteil** is the *subject* and **ist** is the *verb*. If you put some other word, or phrase, at the beginning of the sentence, then the verb and its subject change places. Frau Hansen states her market share in the US thus:

In den USA ist unser Marktanteil 9%

Here is another example:

Der Verkauf ist um 19%   *Sales have risen by 19%*
gestiegen

If we add *in the EC* to the beginning of this sentence, we have:

In der EG ist der Verkauf   *Sales in the EC have risen*
um 19% gestiegen.   *by 19%*

Time expressions often occur at the beginning of a sentence. You may well recall that one of the secretaries in Unit 2 says of the **Exportleiterin**:

Am Donnerstag hat sie   *She has a meeting on Thursday*
eine Konferenz

Adjectives

These are words which answer the question *What sort of ...?* When they stand alone in a sentence the basic form of the adjective is used:

Unser Unternehmen ist mittelgroß   *Our company is medium-sized*

But when they precede a noun they acquire an ending. Callum refers to his *medium-sized family business* as:

ein mittelgroßer Familienbetrieb (masculine)

Frau Hansen's firm is an international company:

ein internationales Unternehmen (neuter)

And earlier Liz responds with the phrase:

eine interessante Frage (feminine)

As you can see, the endings on the adjective are:

-er *(masculine)*; **-es** *(neuter)*; **-e** *(feminine)*

In the plural, the adjective is often used alone before a noun, and in this case it takes an **-e** ending:

hochwertige Strickwaren   *high-quality knitwear*

There is more about this in the *Language reference* section.

Um

You have already come across one meaning of this word when it is used with time:

um 14 Uhr   *at 2 pm*

In Unit 5, we come across the same word with a different meaning. It is used to mean *by*, when saying *by* how much something has increased or decreased:

Der Verkauf ist **um** 15% gestiegen   *Sales have risen **by** 15%*

Am

In the context of dates and days of the week, we came across **am** with the meaning *on* (or *on the*):

am Montag	*on* Monday
am 7. Dezember	*on* the 7th December

In Unit 5 we come across it meaning *of the:*

Unser Anteil **am** italienischen Markt ist um 7% gestiegen	*Our share **of the** Italian market has risen by 7%*

Language map 1

Export markets

Wir haben ein großes Sortiment...

Unser Verkauf ist dieses Jahr um fünfzig Prozent gestiegen...

In Großbritannien, in Italien und in Deutschland geht der Verkauf gut...

Jetzt wollen wir nach Japan exportieren.

Language map 2

Researching the markets

Wieviele Pullover verkaufen Sie pro Monat?

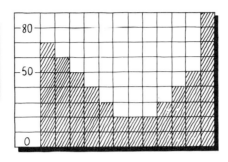

50 oder 60 ungefähr. Im Winter verkaufen wir mehr als im Sommer.

Wer sind die typischen Kunden?

Das sind Berufstätige mit gutem Einkommen im Alter von 25 bis 55 Jahren.

Welche Größen verkaufen sich gut?

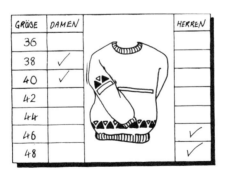

Bei Damenpullovern die Größen 38 und 40 besonders, und bei Herrenpullovern die Größen 46 und 48.

Eignen sich unsere Modelle für den deutschen Markt?

FARBE	PREIS	MODELL	
	✓	✓	GUT
			ZIEMLICH GUT
✓			SCHLECHT

Ja, sehr gut sogar, aber ich möchte andere Farben sehen.

Unit 6 *Eating out with business contacts*

Checklist In this Unit you will learn to:

❏ order food and drink in a restaurant

❏ ask what things are, what is recommended and what is available

❏ say what you like and dislike.

You will also learn some small-talk for the dinner table.

Key words and phrases
for you to use

Asking for help or information

Malteser? Was ist das?	*Malteser? What's that?*
Was für Käse/Wein/ Bier haben Sie?	*What sort of cheese/wine/beer have you got?*
Was empfehlen Sie?	*What do you recommend?*

Ordering and paying

Ich nehme eine Specksuppe	*I'll have ham soup*
Ich möchte ein Filetsteak	*I'd like a fillet steak*
gut durchgebraten	*well done*
halbdurch	*medium*
leicht angebraten	*rare*
die Rechnung, bitte	*the bill, please*
Was macht das?	*How much is that?*

Accepting/refusing

Ja, bitte!	*Yes please!*
Ja schon	*Yes indeed*
Ich möchte schon den Räucherfischteller probieren	*I would like to try the platter of smoked fish*
Danke, ich bin schon satt	*No thank you, I'm full*
Für mich nicht	*Not for me*

Expressing likes and dislikes

Ich mag die deutsche Küche	*I like German cooking*
Ich mag keinen Fisch	*I don't like fish*
Ich nehme lieber die Specksuppe	*I'd prefer the ham soup*
Ich trinke lieber Mineralwasser	*I prefer mineral water*
Ich esse sehr gern Pommes frites	*I love chips*

Small talk

Talking about yourself

Ich bin verheiratet	*I am married*
Ich bin nicht verheiratet	*I'm not married*
Ich bin ledig	*I'm single*
Ich habe zwei Kinder	*I've got two children*
Ich habe keine Kinder	*I've no children*
Ich komme aus Cardiff/ Glasgow	*I'm from Cardiff/Glasgow*
Ich wohne in Dublin	*I live in Dublin*
Ich rauche/ich rauche nicht	*I smoke/I don't smoke*
Ich arbeite seit drei Jahren bei Lehmann und Kraus	*I've been working for Lehmann und Kraus for three years*
Nein, meine Frau arbeitet zur Zeit nicht	*No, my wife doesn't have a job at present*

Talking about the weather

Das Wetter ist schön/heiß/kalt	*It's fine/hot/cold*
Es regnet	*It's raining*

Key words and phrases
for you to recognize

Table talk

Guten Appetit!	*Enjoy your meal!*
Mahlzeit!	*Enjoy your lunch*
Möchten Sie etwas trinken?	*Would you like something to drink?*
Paßt Ihnen dieser Tisch?	*Does this table suit you?*
Die Speisekarte, bitte schön	*Here you are - the menu*
Wollen Sie den Fisch probieren?	*Would you like to try the fish?*
Wollen Sie lieber ein Steak?	*Would you prefer a steak?*
Eine Spezialität des Hauses	*A speciality of the house*
Ich empfehle das Steak	*I recommend the steak*
Das ist eine Spezialität hier bei uns	*That is a speciality here in the area*
Der Wein kommt aus dieser Gegend	*The wine is from this region*
Haben Sie schon gewählt?	*Have you chosen?/Are you ready to order?*
als Vorspeise	*as a starter*
als Hauptgericht	*as a main course*
als Nachspeise	*as dessert*
Hat es Ihnen geschmeckt?	*Did you enjoy your meal?*
Soll ich es Ihnen aufschreiben?	*Shall I put it on the bill?*

Business talk

Gehen die Geschäfte gut?	*Is business going well?*
Wie lange arbeiten Sie schon bei der Firma Klaus Bahr?	*How long have you been with the company Klaus Bahr?*
Sind Sie mit Ihrem Besuch hier bei uns zufrieden?	*Are you pleased with your visit to us?*
Sie fliegen morgen zurück?	*Are you flying back tomorrow?*
Auf unsere Zusammenarbeit!	*To our collaboration!*

Small talk

Kennen Sie Deutschland?	*Do you know Germany?*
Sind Sie zum ersten Mal hier in Hamburg?	*Is this your first time here in Hamburg?*
Woher kommen Sie?	*Where are you from?*
Wo wohnen Sie?	*Where do you live?*
Stört es Sie, wenn ich rauche?	*Do you mind if I smoke?*
Regnet es wirklich so oft in England?	*Does it really rain so much in England?*
Wenn ich es mir erlauben darf ...	*If I may be so bold ...*
Sind Sie verheiratet?	*Are you married?*
Haben Sie Kinder?	*Have you got children?*
nicht mehr	*no longer*
ab und zu	*from time to time*
direkt im Zentrum	*directly in the town centre*
Mein Sohn/Meine Tochter ist ...... Jahre alt	*My son/daughter is .... years old*

1 Listen to the conversation in the restaurant and tick those items you hear mentioned.

Speisekarte

Vorspeisen

Starters

Holsteiner Specksuppe 9.50
Ham soup from Schleßwig Holstein

Tomatencremesuppe mit Gin 10.00
Cream of tomato soup with gin

Räucherfischteller vom Lachs, Aal, und Forellenfilet mit warmer Baguette und Butter 20.80
Platter of smoked fish – salmon, eel, and trout with warm French bread and butter

Tomatensalat mit frischem Basilikum 8.50
Tomato salad with fresh basil

 ## Hauptgerichte

Main courses

Schollenfilet auf Blattspinat mit Sc. Bearnaise und Salzkartoffeln 28.50
Fillet of plaice on a bed of spinach with a French sauce and boiled potatoes

Paniertes Schweineschnitzel mit Erbsen, Möhren, und Pommes Frites 25.60
Pork Schnitzel with peas, carrots, and french fries

Schweinelendchen in Calvadossoße mit glacierten Fingermöhrchen 33.50
Pork loin in Calvados sauce with glazed finger carrots

Filetsteak mit Bratkartoffeln und gemischtem Salat　32.00

Fillet steak with roast potatoes and mixed salad

 Damhirschrücken 'Hubertus' mit Pfifferlingen, Ananasscheiben, gefüllt mit Preiselbeeren　33.50

Venison shoulder Hubertus with chanterelle and pineapple, filled with cranberry sauce.

Zanderfilet gebraten, serviert mit Pfifferlingrahmsoße, Salzkartoffeln, und Kopfsalat　32.00

Perch fillet served with a chanterelle sauce, potatoes, and a green salad

Beilagen

Side dishes

Portion Salzkartoffeln　　　　Portion Pommes Frites

Boiled potatoes　　　　　　　　French fries

Portion Bratkartoffeln

Fried potatoes

Nachspeisen

Desserts

Rote Grütze mit flüßiger Sahne　8.50

Speciality red jelly with single cream

Jan im Sack~Apfelbeignets in Bierteig gebacken mit Vanillesoße　8.00

Jan in a sack - apple fritters with a vanilla sauce

Mousse au chocolat　7.50

Gemischtes Eis (Schokolade, Vanille, Erdbeer)　6.00

Ice-cream - chocolate, vanilla, strawberry

Käseauswahl, mit Brot, Butter und Oliven　10.50

Selection of cheeses with bread butter and olives

2   Listen to the conversations between Liz and Herr Buhtz and Jim and Frau Borm and answer the following questions.

1   What age are Jim's children?

    a) 11, 8 and 5 years of age

    b) 11, 8 and 4 years of age

    c) 12, 9 and 7 years of age

2   He has

    a) 3 boys

    b) a boy and 2 girls

    c) 2 boys and a girl

3   How long has Jim been with Thermoglaze?

    a) 3 years

    b) 2 years

    c) 12 years

4   What is his wife's job?

    a) Secretary

    b) Marketing Director

    c) Personnel Manager

5   How many children has Herr Buhtz?

    a) 2

    b) none

    c) 3

6   What ages are Liz's children?

    a) 8 and 16 years of age

    b) 18 and 5 years of age

    c) 8 and 15 years of age

Languagemap

Wollen Sie etwas trinken?

Ja, bitte.

Wollen Sie eine Spezialität des Hauses probieren?

Ja schon. Was empfehlen Sie?

Mögen Sie Suppe? Die Specksuppe ist sehr gut.

Ja, ich mag Specksuppe sehr gern.

Und danach - ich empfehle den Zander.

Zander - was ist das?

Das ist ein Fisch - eine Spezialität hier.

Es tut mir leid. Ich mag keinen Fisch.

Ein Steak dann? Mögen Sie Ihr Steak gut durchgebraten oder halbdurch?

Leicht angebraten, bitte.

Etwas später

Gehen die Geschäfte gut?

Ja, ja sehr gut, danke.

Wie lange arbeiten Sie schon bei Thermoglaze?

Seit 3 Jahren.

Sind Sie mit Ihrem Besuch hier bei uns zufrieden, Herr Reade?

Sehr zufrieden! Auf unsere Zusammenarbeit!

Möchten Sie einen Schnaps ?

Ja, eigentlich schon.

Was für Schnaps haben Sie?

Wir haben Branntwein, Malteser,...

Ich nehme einen Branntwein, bitte.

Und eine Zigarre?

Nein danke, ich bin Nichtraucher.

Wenn ich es mir erlauben darf... sind Sie verheiratet?

Ja, ich bin verheiratet.

Haben Sie Kinder?

Nein, ich habe keine Kinder.

Woher kommen Sie?

Ich komme aus Winchester.

Regnet es wirklich so oft bei Ihnen?

Ja, es regnet viel.

Likes and dislikes

If you are discussing the menu before ordering you may be asked:

Mögen Sie ......?   *Do you like ......?*

To which you reply:

Ja, ich mag/Nein, ich   *Yes, I like/No, I don't*
mag ...   *like ...*

keinen Fisch (masculine)   *fish*

keine Suppe (feminine)   *soup*

kcin Eis (neuter)   *ice cream*

Saying what you'll have

The host, or waiter might ask you to have something with the phrase:

Was möchten Sie?   *What would you like?*

Was nehmen Sie?   *What will you have?*

Your reply might then be:

Ich möchte, or **ich nehme einen Sherry** (masculine), **eine Suppe** (feminine), or **ein Bier** (neuter)

To say what you'd prefer you can add **lieber**:

Ich nehme lieber Fleisch   *I'd prefer meat*

Checking what is available

If you want to check what selection is available, you can ask:

Was für ......?   *What sort of ......?*

Was für Saft haben Sie?   *What kind of juice have you got?*

Doing business in Germany

German business style tends to be quite formal, although this is changing somewhat amongst younger executives.

Dos and Don'ts

Do shake hands when meeting someone and again when taking leave. This is a ritual that is repeated at every meeting, even amongst business colleagues who see each other every day. If there are a number of people present, go round everyone or risk being considered rude.

Don't use first names. Address your business acquaintance as 'Herr X' or 'Frau Y'. Even people who have worked together for years use this formal form of address in Germany. Sometimes an acquaintance might suggest you begin to call each other 'du', i.e. use the informal form of address together with first names, in which case you should reciprocate. An earlier rather than a later transition to 'du' terms is becoming more common in Germany, particularly amongst the younger generation.

Do be prepared to start work early. Work begins in Germany at any time from 7 am onwards. So 9–10 am is already mid-morning, and lunch is normally between noon and 1 pm.

Do expect your German customer to demand quality and punctual delivery. In the past Britain hasn't had a very good reputation in the Federal Republic in this respect. German industry has built its export success on these factors and expects the same from its suppliers.

Do expect to have to work hard to get into the German market. It's a demanding market which requires good preparation and persistence, but is rewarding if you succeed. You can find help and advice about doing business in Germany from the Department of Trade and Industry, the German Chamber of Commerce in London, the Embassy of the Federal Republic of Germany and British commercial representatives in Germany.

Don't forget to take a small gift if invited home by a business colleague. It's normal to take flowers, but something typically British is also appreciated.

What next?

Here are some further suggestions for improving your German and your knowledge of Germany.

Enrol for some language training to supplement your private study. Even a small number of hours of tuition will boost your confidence and allow you to clarify any points that may have been troubling you. Your local college or polytechnic may run courses for business people or offer tutor support, on a one-to-one basis, for students using open-learning packs like **German *Just for Business***. The Goethe Institutes in London, Birmingham and Manchester, and the Scottish German Centre in Glasgow run courses, and there are also many private organizations offering language training. The Association of Language Export Centres (Tel. 071-224 3748) is a useful source of information on good quality language training.

Listen to the German radio, for example *Deutschlandfunk* and *Deutsche Welle*. If you have satellite TV with the right aerial there are several German language stations, such as *Sat1*, *3Sat* or some of the German regional stations, which you can receive.

Buy a German newspaper from time to time, such as the *Frankfurter Allgemeine Zeitung*, or a magazine like *Stern* or the business weekly *Wirtschaftswoche*. Even if you can only under-stand the headlines or the gist of the articles you will acquire some useful vocabulary.

Improve your background knowledge of Germany by working your way through a software package on doing business with the Germans called *Getting Down to Business with Germany* (obtain-able from Lloyds Insurance Training Centre or by reading the Country Profile on Germany published by the DTI (Exports to Europe Branch, Department of Trade and Industry, 1 Victoria Street, London SW1H 0ET). *Mind Your Manners*, published by the Industrial Society, is another useful source of information.

Viel Glück!

Answers to exercises

Unit 1

1 1.c.   2.a.   3.d.   4.b.

2 1. Beckmann, Köln (Cologne)   2. Neusiedler, München
(Munich)

3 1. True   2. True   3. False   4. False

4 This afternoon would be the best time to phone, since Herr
Henschel is in Berlin tomorrow when you're free and you're in
Le Havre on Wednesday when he is free.

Unit 2

1 Telephone and fax numbers
1. 31 05 83   2. 53 39 065   3. 36 34 04   4. 66 03 94

1 and 3 are correct and 2 and 4 have changed.

3 1. Cii   2. Aiii   3. Biv

4 1. There is a mistake here: It is Karl Habermann from the
company Eggers. It's about a meeting, next week on 22nd.
October.

2. There is information omitted here: The meeting tomorrow
with Herr Ehrlich, the Export Director, is cancelled.

3. There is a mistake here: Karin Lehmann is arriving on
Tuesday at 13.20 at Heathrow. Her flight number is LH
254.

Unit 3

1 1. Herr Papst from the Production Department is expecting
Herr Schmidt from BASF at 10.30.

2. Frau Raetz from the Marketing Department is expecting
Frau Kupelwieser from an Advertising Agency at 11.00.

3. Herr Dieter from the Purchasing Department is expecting
Frau Grünewald from Mannesmann at 11.30.

4. Herr Martens from the Accounts Department is expecting Herr Breuer from Kunz at 11.30.

2 The correct order is:

G, C, A, F, D, H, B, E.

Unit 4

1 1. A high quality product 2. Modern and practical 3. Easy to install. The feature omitted is: "It is a popular model"

2 1. The round windows are 80 cms and 110 cms

2. The crate is 90 cm long, 70 cm across and 50 cm high.

3. Both writing desks are 72 cm high. The large one is 75 cm across and 145 cm long. The small one is 65 cm across and 130 cm long.

4. The large paper plate is 28 cm in diameter. The others are 23 cm and 18 cm.

Unit 5

1 Your notes on Helga Hansen's company should include the following:

Founded: 12 years ago

Head office: Munich

Factories: Italy, Portugal, Germany

Number of employees: 680

Turnover: 560 Million DM

Current markets: Europe and USA

Future plans: Export to France

Your notes on Klaus Wickmann's company should include:

Founded: 10 years ago

Foreign branches: France (Grenoble), Italy (Mailand/Milan), UK (London)

Number of employees: 150 in Germany and 220 abroad

Turnover: 530 Million DM

2 Your bar chart should contain the following information:

Market share	*Rise in sales*
Internal Mkt 20%	8%
USA 9%	20%
EC 4%	12%

3 Your notes should contain the following information:

AF89
Yes, in stock,
Delivery time is 2 weeks
Price is 160DM

AZ47
No, only made to order.
Delivery time is 6 weeks
Price is 230DM

Discount 2% on orders over 20,000DM; 5% on orders over 50,000DM
Payment against invoice.

Unit 6

1 The dishes chosen were:

As starters, Specksuppe and Räucherfischteller
As main course, Filetsteak and Zander.

2 1. a.   2. c   3.a   4. b   5. b   6.c

Language reference

Pronunciation guide

This section is designed to supplement the tape pronunciation guide that follows the introduction on cassette one.

Three key things to practise

German pronunciation does not present any major difficulties for the learner. Many people, indeed, find it easier than French. It is important, however, that you are aware of how the pure German vowels are sounded, that you practise the two umlaut sounds and the consonant sounds which we don't have in English (these are described below), and that you produce nice, clear consonants which are not slurred. If you can do these three things, then you shouldn't have too many problems.

Using the tape

It is absolutely vital that when practising the pronunciation you take every opportunity to repeat the words on the tape. Very often there is a space for you to repeat a new word, but even where we haven't left a space, make sure that you use your pause button and rewind, to say the word and get it absolutely right.

Repeating after the tape and pronunciation practice should always be done aloud: saying it silently is not enough, because your mouth and tongue need the practice too.

The German vowel sounds

If you are from northern Britain you will find the German vowel sounds easier. They are best likened to the Scottish pure, open vowels. The way a Scot would pronounce the word man, is the same as the German pronunciation in Mann. If you are from the South you will need to practise this.

-i   In the middle of the word it is like the English -i in *kiss*, a bit short and sharp. Listen to the word **bitte**, *(please)* on the tape.

-e   Every **-e** at the end of the word is sounded. Listen again to the word **bitte** in Unit 1.

-ei   These vowels often come together in the middle of a word. They are always sounded like the English *eye*. It is quite a familiar sound, but you can practise it if you listen to the word **mein** *(my)*.

-ie In the middle of the word this is always pronounced like an English -ee. You will come across it in the German word **hier** *(here)*.

-a The German word **Name** has the same spelling as the English equivalent, but practise the pure open **-a** in the middle. The **-e** at the end sounds like the *i* in *third*. Compare it to the word **Firma**, company, where the final sound is open and round.

-u This sound is like the English -*oo*. You can practise it in the word **gut** *(good)*.

-eu Pronounce this combination like *oy* in *boy*.

The umlaut

This consists of two dots above the vowels **-a, -o, -u** (ä, ö, ü) which indicate that the vowel has a slightly different sound from usual.

-ä This is a rather familiar sound, like the vowels in the English word *air*. You will hear it in the German word **später**.

-ö This is a sound which we don't have in English. You will hear it in the words **möchte** and **könnte** in the first Unit, so try practising these on your tape.

-ü This is also a new sound for English speakers. You will hear it in the German word **zurück** *(back)*, which you can practise saying after the tape.

-äu Also sounds like the English *oy*.

The consonants

Most of the sounds here are familiar, but we need to be aware of a few differences in pronunciation.

-j is pronounced like an English -(-y). You can practise this in the German words **ja** *(yes)* and **Jahr** *(year)*.

-s is pronounced like an English -z. Practise the word for *engaged*, **besetzt**.

—v as in **vier** sounds like an English *f*, whereas

—w is pronounced like an English *v*. Now trying saying **Volkswagen**.

-z is pronounced as a **-ts**. Listen for it in the German for *ten*, **zehn**.

-qu is slightly different from the English. It is more like a **- kv**. You will hear a good deal about quality products in the book, so you can practise it in the German word **Qualität**.

sp- and **st-** at the beginning of a word are pronounced **schp-** and **scht**. **Der Sport** (the same word in German) becomes **Schport**. You can hear this too in the word **sprechen** *(to speak)*.

A rather more difficult sound for the southern British is **-ch**. This is like the Scottish *loch*. You will hear it in the word for *to spell*, **buchstabieren**.

A slightly different, softer **-ch** is in the word for *I*, **ich**. The sound here is a bit like the English -h in *huge*.

The alphabet

You can read this section as you listen to the alphabet on the tape. Try sounding the letters as follows:

a *ah,*   **b** *bay,*   **c** *tsay,*   **d** *day,*   **e** *ay,*   **f** *eff,*   **g** *gay,*
h *ha,*   **i** *ee,*   **j** *yot,*   **k** *ka,*   **l** *ell,* **m** *emm,*   **n** *enn,*
o *oh,*   **p** *pay,*   **q** *cou,*   **r** *err,*   **s** *ess,* **t** *tay,*   **u** *ooh,*
v *fow,* **w** *vay,*   **x** *iks,*   **y** *üpsilon,* **z** *tsett*

The declension of the definite article (der, die, das)

There is a form of the word *the* for each of the three different genders. The plural is the same for all genders.

When the noun accompanying *the* is the subject of the sentence, or clause, it is in the nominative case.

Nominative (the subject):

	Singular	**Plural**
Masculine	der Besuch	die Besuche
	(the visit)	*(the visits)*
Feminine	die Besprechung	die Besprechungen
	(the meeting)	*(the meetings)*
Neuter	das Angebot	die Angebote
	(the offer)	*(the offers)*

When the noun is the object of the sentence, then it is said to be in the Accusative. The masculine form changes.

Accusative (the object):

	Singular	**Plural**
Masculine	den Besuch	die Besuche
	(the visit)	*(the visits)*
Feminine	die Besprechung	die Besprechungen
	(the meeting)	*(the meetings)*
Neuter	das Angebot	die Angebote
	(the offer)	*(the offers)*

The declension of the indefinite article (ein, eine)

There are a number of words which have the same declension as **ein**. The ones which occur in this course are: **mein** *(my)*, **Ihr** *(your)*, **unser** *(our)*, **kein** *(none, no)*.

Nominative (the subject):

	Singular	
Masculine	ein Schreibtisch	*a desk*
Feminine	eine Konferenz	*a meeting*
Neuter	ein Büro	*an office*

The plural is the same for all genders:

Plural	meine Konferenzen	*my meetings*

Accusative (the object):

Again, in the Accusative, it is only the masculine which changes:

Masculine	einen Schreibtisch	*a desk*
Feminine	eine Konferenz	*a meeting*
Neuter	ein Büro	*an office*
Plural	meine Konferenzen	*my meetings*

The declension of the adjective with the definite article

When *the* is followed by an adjective, or describing word, the adjective also takes an ending. Once again the plural is the same for all genders.

Nominative (the subject):

Masculine	der interessante Besuch	*the interesting visit*
Feminine	die lange Besprechung	*the long meeting*
Neuter	das gute Angebot	*the good offer*
Plural	die interessanten Besuche	*the interesting visits*

When the adjective is in the Accusative Case, as the object, then as with the nouns, only the masculine changes:

Accusative (the object):

Masculine	den interessanten Besuch	*the interesting visit*
Feminine	die lange Besprechung	*the long meeting*
Neuter	das gute Angebot	*the good offer*
Plural	die interessanten Besuche	*the interesting visits*

The declension of the adjective with the indefinite article

Compare the following endings on the adjective with those above - they are quite different. In grammatical parlance we say that these are strong endings. Note how they reflect gender more 'strongly'.

Nominative (the subject):

Masculine	ein großer Schreibtisch	*a large desk*
Feminine	eine späte Konferenz	*a late meeting*
Neuter	ein kleines Büro	*a small office*
Plural	meine späten Konferenzen	*my late meetings*

Accusative (the object):

Masculine	einen großen Schreibtisch	*a large desk*
Feminine	eine späte Konferenz	*a late meeting*
Neuter	ein kleines Büro	*a small office*
Plural	meine späten Konferenzen	*my late meetings*

Nouns

All nouns in German are written with an initial capital letter:

das Telefon   *The telephone*

Feminine forms

In German, many names for jobs, or words referring to persons, are normally masculine, but can be made into a feminine form simply by adding - **in** to the noun:

der Kollege	*the colleague*
die Kollegin	*the colleague (female)*
der Verkaufsleiter	*the sales director*
die Verkaufsleiterin	*the sales director (female)*

Plurals

There are several different ways of forming plurals in German. The plural form is given in brackets after the noun in all good, modern dictionaries and, for this course, they can be checked easily in the glossary.

Below is a list of ways in which plurals can be formed for each gender. The list is not exhaustive, but the most common plural forms are featured in the order of frequency with which they occur. As you will notice, the plural form sometimes takes an umlaut over the central vowel in the word.

Masculine
1 ("e)   2 (-e)   3 (-(e)n)

Feminine
1 (-(e)n)   2 ("e)

Neuter
1 ("er)   2 (-)   3 (-e)

Compound nouns

In German one compound noun can act as a substitute for an English phrase. These compounds are formed by putting together two or more words (compounds with three or four are quite common). The last word is always a noun and it also determines the gender. The English language no longer has this facility, although Welsh still does!

An example from your tape is:

der Spielwarenhersteller   *toy manufacturer*

It's made up of the verb **spielen** *to play,* **Waren** *goods* and **Hersteller** *manufacturer*

Weak and strong verbs

Regular or weak verbs

These always take the endings below, and do not otherwise change. If a verb does not figure in the list of strong verbs in your dictionary, then you apply this standard weak conjugation.

bestätigen	*to confirm*
ich bestätige	*I confirm*
er, sie, es bestätigt	*he, she, it confirms*
wir bestätigen	*we confirm*
Sie, sie bestätigen	*you, they confirm*

Irregular or strong verbs

These usually have a change in the central vowel of the verb stem. (This may not be in the present tense; it may only occur when the verb is put into the past). In the present tense, the pattern of endings remains the same as above.

sprechen	*to speak*
ich spreche	*I speak*
er, sie, es spricht	*he, she, it speaks*
wir sprechen	*we speak*
Sie, sie sprechen	*you, they speak*

Sein *(to be)*, haben *(to have)*

These verbs are irregular.

sein *(to be)*		**haben** *(to have)*	
ich bin	*I am*	ich habe	*I have*
er, sie, es ist	*he, she, it is*	er, sie, es hat	*he, she, it has*
wir sind	*we are*	wir haben	*we have*
Sie, sie sind	*you, they are*	Sie, sie haben	*you, they have*

The modal verbs

Mögen *(to like to)*, können *(to be able to)*, müssen *(to have to)*, wollen *(to want to)*, dürfen *(to be allowed to)*, sollen *(to be supposed to)*. These six verbs usually occur with another verb. This second verb comes at the end of the sentence, as in the following example:

Ich **möchte** bitte Herrn Buhtz **sprechen**

mögen

ich mag	*I like (to)*
er, sie, es mag	*he, she, it likes (to)*
wir mögen	*we like (to)*
Sie, sie mögen	*you, they like (to)*

können

ich kann	*I can/am able to*
er, sie, es kann	*he, she, it can/is able to*
wir können	*we can/are able to*
Sie, sie können	*you, they can/are able to*

müssen

ich muß	*I must/have to*
er, sie, es muß	*he, she, it must/has to*
wir müssen	*we must/have to*
Sie, sie müssen	*you, they must/have to*

wollen

ich will	*I want to*
er, sie, es will	*he, she, it wants to*
wir wollen	*we want to*
Sie, sie wollen	*you, they want to*

dürfen

ich darf	*I may/am allowed to*
er, sie, es darf	*he, she, it may/is allowed to*
wir dürfen	*we may/are allowed to*
Sie, sie dürfen	*you, they may/are allowed to*

sollen

ich soll	*I am supposed to*
er, sie, es soll	*he, she, it is supposed to*
wir sollen	*we are supposed to*
Sie, sie sollen	*you, they are supposed to*

The conditional tense (polite form)

Three of the above modals occur frequently in the conditional tense.

mögen

ich möchte	*I would like (to)*
er, sie, es möchte	*he, she, it would like (to)*
wir möchten	*we would like (to)*
Sie, sie möchten	*you, they would like (to)*

The verbs **können** and **dürfen** also follow this pattern of endings in the conditional tense:

können

ich könnte	*I could/would be able to, etc*

dürfen

ich dürfte	*I might/may be allowed to, etc*

The separable verbs

The common separable verbs which occur on your tape are **zurückrufen** *(to phone back)*, **anrufen** *(to phone)*, **herstellen** *(to manufacture)*, **anbieten** *(to offer)*.

These are verbs with a prefix which separates from the main part of the verb, when it is used as the main verb of a sentence:

Ich rufe Frau Fuchs morgen wieder an	*I'll phone Frau Fuchs again tomorrow*

or when you use it to give an order or command:

Rufen Sie später zurück!	*Phone back later!*

The separable verb with a modal

In this case the separable verb is written as one word and comes at the end of the sentence in the infinitive:

Ich möchte Frau Fuchs morgen zurückrufen	*I'd like to phone Frau Fuchs back tomorrow*

Reflexive verbs

'Reflexive' means that the object of the verb is the same as the subject. Such verbs occur more frequently in German than in English and they are dealt with in some detail in Unit 5.

The reflexive verbs which occur on your tape are **sich spezialisieren** *(to specialize)*, **sich eignen** *(to be suited)*, and **sich verkaufen** *(to sell)*.

sich eignen	to be suited
ich eigne **mich**	*I am suited*
er, sie, es eignet **sich**	*s/he, it is suited*
wir eignen **uns**	*we are suited*
Sie, sie eignen **sich**	*you, they are suited*

Watch out for the variation in word order of the question form with reflexives:

Eignen sie sich gut?	*Are they well suited (appropriate)?*
Eignen sich diese Modelle gut?	*Are these models well suited (appropriate)?*

The days of the week

Montag	Freitag
Dienstag	Samstag *(or* Sonnabend)
Mittwoch	Sonntag
Donnerstag	
am Montag	*on Monday*

The months

Januar	Juli
Februar	August
März	September
April	Oktober
Mai	November
Juni	Dezember

The cardinal numbers

1	eins	11	elf	21	einundzwanzig
2	zwei (zwo)	12	zwölf	22	zweiundzwanzig
3	drei	13	dreizehn	23	dreiundzwanzig
4	vier	14	vierzehn	24	vierundzwanzig
5	fünf	15	fünfzehn	25	fünfundzwanzig
6	sechs	16	sechzehn	26	sechsundzwanzig
7	sieben	17	siebzehn	27	siebenundzwanzig
8	acht	18	achtzehn	28	achtundzwanzig
9	neun	19	neunzehn	29	neunundzwanzig
10	zehn	20	zwanzig		

30	dreißig
40	vierzig
50	fünfzig
60	sechzig
70	siebzig
80	achtzig
90	neunzig

100	hundert
1 000	tausend
1 000 000	cine Million

Larger numbers are written as one word:
hundertneunundneunzig (199)

The ordinal numbers: first, second, third . . .

These are particularly important for the date.

der erste	*the first*
der zweite	*the second*
der dritte	*the third*

From 4th to 19th, just add **-te** to the cardinal number.

der elfte, der siebzehnte

But note: **sieben** *seven*, **siebte** *seventh*.

From 20th onwards, add **-ste** to the basic number:

der vierundzwanzigste, der neunundachtzigste

Telling the time (die Uhrzeit)

Wieviel Uhr ist es?	*What time is it?*
Es ist elf Uhr	*It's 11 o'clock*

The half hour is expressed in German as *half before*:

Es ist halb zehn	*It is half past nine*

The Germans frequently use the 24 hour clock in business.

Es ist dreizehn Uhr	*It's one o'clock*
Es ist fünfzehn Uhr fünfzehn	*It's three fifteen*
Es ist zehn Uhr vierundfünfzig	*It's ten forty-five*
Es ist sechzehn Uhr dreißig	*It's four thirty*
Um wieviel Uhr ist die Besprechung?	*What time is the meeting?*
Um vierzehn Uhr	*At 2 pm*

Vocabulary

Notes

1 Abbreviations:

adj.	adjective	*pron.*	pronoun
adv.	adverb	*sep.*	separable verb
inf.	informal	*s.o.*	someone
jdm.	jemandem (someone)	*str.*	strong verb
pl.	plural	*tel.*	telephone
prep.	preposition		

2 Gender of nouns is indicated by the definite article, i.e. **der** (*masculine*), **die** (*feminine*), **das** (*neuter*).

3 Masculine and feminine forms of nouns relating to people are indicated as follows:

der/die Abteilungsleiter/in

i.e. *masculine:* **der** Abteilungsleit**er**
feminine: **die** Abteilungsleit**erin**

4 Plural forms of nouns are shown in brackets, e.g.

die Adresse (**-n**)

i.e. *singular:* die Adresse
plural: die Adresse**n**

German - English

A

aber but
absagen *sep.* to cancel (appointment)
die **Abteilung** (-en) department
der/die **Abteilungsleiter/in** head of department
ab und zu occasionally
die **Adresse** (-n) address
die **Aktentasche** (-n) briefcase
alles everything
als when; as; than
also so; Well, ...
alt old
älter older
das **Alter** age
das **Aluminium** aluminium
am at the; on the

der/die **Amerikaner/in** American (citizen)
amerikanisch American *adj.*
an at; on
anbieten *sep.; str.* to offer
andere(r,s) other; different
ändern to change
das **Angebot** (-e) offer
der **Anschluß** (Anschlüsse) tel. line
der **Anteil** (an) share (of)
der **Apfelsaft** apple juice
der **Apparat** (-e) telephone; apparatus
der **Appetit** appetite
arbeiten to work
auch too; also
auf on; to
auflösen *sep.* to cancel (contract)
aufschreiben *sep.; str.* to put on the bill
der **Augenblick** (-e) moment

aus *prep.* from (a place);
  made of
die **Ausführung** (-en) design;
  finish; model
im Ausland abroad
etwas ausrichten *sep.* to leave a
  message
das **Auto** (-s) car

B

badisch from the Baden area
die **Banküberweisung** (-en) bank
  transfer
die **Baufirma** (-firmen) building
  company
der **Baumarkt** (-märkte) builders'
  merchant
behilflich helpful
bei Ihnen at/to your place/home/
  company
bei uns at/to our place/home/
  company
beide both
Beispiel: zum Beispiel for example
bekommen *str.* to get; receive
  er bekommt ... he'll have ...
beliebt popular
berufstätig working; in employment
beschäftigen to employ
beschäftigt busy (person)
der **Bescheid** information
  jdm. Bescheid sagen to inform s.o.;
  let s.o. know
besetzt *tel.* busy; engaged
besonders especially
die **Besprechung** (-en) meeting
besser better
bestätigen to confirm
bestellen to order
die **Bestellnummer** (-n) order number
die **Bestellung** (-en) order
  auf Bestellung produzieren to make
  to order
der **Besuch** (-e) visit
betragen *str.* to amount to
das **Bier** beer
der **Bierkenner** (-) connoisseur of beer
bis until
bitte please; don't mention it!
bitte schön! here you are!, don't
  mention it!
bleiben *str.* to remain; stay
breit wide

der **Brief** (-e) letter
  per Brief by letter
bringen to bring
britisch British
die **Broschüre** (-n) brochure
das **Brot** bread
  buchstabieren to spell
das **Büro** (-s) office
die **Butter** butter

D

da there
der **Damenpullover** (-) woman's sweater
danke (no) thank you
danken to thank
dann then
das the; it; that
das **Datum** (Daten) date
denken to think
das **Deutsch** German (language)
deutsch *adj.* German
der/die **Deutsche** German (citizen)
Deutschland Germany
diese(r,s) this; these
direkt direct(ly)
dort there
dringend urgent
durchgebraten well done (of steak)
der **Durchmesser** (-) diameter
dürfen to be allowed to; may
darf may; is/are allowed to

E

die **EDV** electronic data-processing
die **EDV-Abteilung** Computer
  Department
die **EG** EC
eher rather
sich **eignen für** to be suitable for
der **Einkauf** (-käufe) purchase
die **Einkaufsabteilung** Purchasing
  Department
der/die **Einkaufsleiter/in** Purchasing
  Manager
das **Einkommen** income
das **Eis** ice(-cream)
der **Empfang** reception desk
empfehlen *str.* to recommend
England England
das **Englisch** English (language)
Entschuldigung! I beg your pardon!

entsprechen *str.* to correspond to
er he
die **Erdbeere** (-n) strawberry
erfolgreich successful
erlauben to allow
erreichen to reach; get in touch with
das **Ersatzteil** (-e) spare part
erteilen to give; hand over to
erwarten to expect
erzählen to tell
essen *str.* to eat
etwas *pron.* something; *adv.* a little;
   somewhat
etwas später a bit later
Europa Europe
europäisch European
existieren to exist
der **Export** (-e) export
die **Exportabteilung** Export Department
exportieren to export

F

die **Fabrik** (-en) factory
der **Familienbetrieb** (-e) family firm
die **Farbe** (-n) colour
der **Farbstreifen** (-) shade card
das **Faß** (Fässer) barrel
   vom Faß from the barrel; draught
fein fine
das **Fenster** (-) window
die **Finanzabteilung** finance department
die **Firma** (-en) firm; company
der **Fisch** fish
die **Flasche** (-n) bottle
das **Flaschenbier** bottled beer
das **Fleisch** meat
die **Frage** (-n) question
fragen to ask
Frankreich France
die **Frau** (-en) woman; Mrs; Miss; Ms
Fräulein! waitress!
frei free
frei Haus carriage paid
freuen to please
freut mich! pleased to meet you!
frisch fresh
für for

G

ganz *adj.* whole; *adv.* quite
garantieren to guarantee

gar nicht not at all
der **Gastwirt** (-e) restaurant proprietor
geben *str.* to give
gebraten roast; fried
gegen against
die **Gegend** (-en) area; district
gehen *str.* to go
es **geht** it's possible; things
   aren't too bad; I'm OK
es **geht um ...** it's about ...
es **geht mir gut** I'm fine.
wie **geht es Ihnen?** how are you?
genau exact(ly)
gern(e) willingly
die **Geschäfte** *pl.* business
der/die **Geschäftsführer/in** Managing
   Director
die **Geschäftsreise** (-n) business trip
geschmeckt tasted (good)
gestiegen increased
gewählt chosen
gibt: es gibt there is; there are
das **Glas** glass
die **Glasstärke** thickness of glass
glauben to think; believe
das **Glück** luck
groß big; large
Großbritannien Great Britain
die **Größe** (-n) size
gut good; fine; well
guten Appetit! enjoy your meal!

H

haben to have
halb *adj.* half
halbdurch medium (steak)
hallo! *inf.* hello!
das **Handbuch** (-bücher) handbook
das **Hauptgericht** (-e) main course
der **Hauptsitz** headquarters
das **Haus** (Häuser) house; building; office
heißen *str.* to be called
das **heißt** that means; that is; i.e.
helfen *str.* to help
der **Herr** (-n, -en) man; Mr
   meine Herrschaften! ladies and
   gentlemen!
der **Herrenpullover** (-) man's sweater
herstellen *sep.* to produce; manufacture
heute today
heute nachmittag this afternoon
heute vormittag this morning
hier here

hinausschieben *sep. str.* to postpone
hoch high; tall
höchst highest
hochwertig high quality
holländisch Dutch
das **Holz** wood

I

ihn him; it
Ihnen (to/for) you
Ihr(e) your
in in; into
die **Industrie** (-n) industry
der/die **Ingenieur/in** engineer
im **Inland** in the home market
insgesamt all together
interessant interesting
international international
Italien Italy
italienisch *adj.* Italian

J

ja yes
ja, bitte/gern yes, please
das **Jahr** (-e) year
jetzt now
der **Junge** (-n) boy

K

der **Kaffee** coffee
der **Kalender** (-) diary
die **Karte** (-n) (business) card
der **Käse** cheese
die **Käseauswahl** selection of cheeses
die **Käsesorte** (-n) type of cheese
der **Katalog** (-e) catalogue
kaufen to buy
kein/e no; not a; not any
kennen to know; be acquainted with
das **Kind** (-er) child
die **Kiste** (-n) crate
klein small; little
der **Kollege/die Kollegin** colleague
kommen *str.* to come
das **kommt darauf an** that all depends
die **Konferenz** (-en) meeting; conference
die **Konkurrenz** competition
können can; to be able
kann can; is/are able

könnte(n) could
das **Konto** (Konten) (bank) account
kosten to cost
krank ill
die **Küche** (-n) kitchen; cuisine
der **Kunde** (-n); **die Kundin** (-nen) customer
der **Kunststoff** (-e) plastic

L

das **Lager** (-) store
auf Lager in store; in stock
der **Lagerartikel** (-) item in stock
das **Lammfleisch** lamb
das **Land** (Länder) country
lang long
lange for a long time
ledig single; unmarried
leicht easy
letzt last
lieber preferably
der **Lieferant** (-en) supplier
die **Lieferbedingungen** *pl.* terms of supply
liefern to supply
die **Lieferzeit** (-en) delivery time
links on the left

M

machen to make; do
das **macht nichts** that doesn't matter
was macht das? what does that come to?
das **Mädchen** (-) girl
die **Mahlzeit** meal
Mahlzeit! enjoy your lunch!
Mailand Milan
mal times; by (dimensions)
das **Mal** (-e) time; occasion
man *pron.* one
das **Marketing** marketing
die **Marketing-Abteilung** Marketing Department
der/die **Marketing-Leiter/in** Marketing Manager
der **Markt** (Märkte) market
der **Marktanteil** (-e) market share
die **Maschine** (-n) machine
das **Material** (-ien) material
das **Maß** (-e) measurement; dimension
mehr more
mein(e) my

meinen to mean; think; be of the opinion
mich me
die **Milch** milk
der/das **Millimeter** (-) millimetre
das **Mineralwasser** mineral water
minus minus
mir me; to me
das **Mißverständnis** (-se) misunderstanding
mit with
der/die **Mitarbeiter/in** employee
mittelgroß medium-sized
mittlere middle; medium
das **Modell** (-e) model
modern modern
mögen to like
mag like(s)
möchte(n) would like
möglich possible
der **Moment** (-e) moment
im Moment at the moment
der **Monat** (-e) month
montieren to install
der **Morgen** (-) morning
morgen tomorrow
morgen vormittag tomorrow morning
müde tired
München Munich
das **Muster** (-) sample

N

nach after; to (with place names)
der **Nachmittag** (-e) afternoon
die **Nachspeise** (-n) dessert
nächst next
der **Name** (-n, -n) name; surname
natürlich naturally; of course
nehmen *str.* to take; have (to eat/drink)
nein no
neu new
nicht not
nicht wahr? isn't that so?
der **Nichtraucher** (-) non-smoker
nichts nothing
nichts zu danken! don't mention it!
die **Niederlande** *pl.* the Netherlands
die **Niederlassung** (-en) branch (of company)
noch still
noch besser als even better than
noch etwas something/anything else

die **Norm** (-en) norm; standard
normalerweise usually
notieren to note
die **Nudeln** *pl.* noodles
die **Nummer** (-n) number
nun now
nur only

O

oder or
ohne without
der **Orangensaft** orange juice
die **Ordnung** order
in **Ordnung!** all right! fine! OK!
originell original; distinctive

P

der **Pappteller** (-) paper plate
passen to suit
das **Pfund** pound (sterling; weight)
das **Plastik** plastic
der **Platz** (Plätze) place; seat
plus plus
die **Pommes frites** *pl.* potato chips
praktisch practical
der **Preis** (-e) price
die **Preisliste** (-n) price list
pro per
probieren to try (out)
das **Problem** (-e) problem
das **Produkt** (-e) product
die **Produktion** production
die **Produktionsabteilung** Production Department
produzieren to produce
das **Prozent** percent
der **Pullover** (-) jumper
putzen to clean

Q

die **Qualität** quality

R

der **Rabatt** (-e) discount (on quantity)
rauchen to smoke
die **Rechnung** (-en) bill
die **Rechnungsabteilung** Accounts Department

rechts on the right
die **Reise** (-n) journey
relativ relatively
richtig right; correct
der **Rotwein** red wine
rufen *str.* to call
rund round

S

der **Saft** (Säfte) juice
sagen to say
sagen wir ... let's say ...
sagen Sie, ... tell me, ...
salopp casual
satt replete; full (up)
der **Schnaps** schnapps; spirits
die **Schokolade** chocolate
schon already; really (emphatic)
die **Schönheitsprodukte** *pl.* beauty
    products
schottisch *adj.* Scottish
Schottland Scotland
schreiben *str.* to write
der **Schreibtisch** (-e) desk
das **Schwein** (-e) pig
sehen *str.* to see
sehr very
sein to be
  ich bin I am
  er/sie/es ist he/she/it is
  wir/Sie/sie sind we/you/they are
seit for; since (time phrases)
die **Sekretärin** (-nen) secretary
sicherlich no doubt
sie *sing.* she; it
sie *pl.* they
Sie you
das **Skonto** (Skonti) discount (for cash or
    prompt payment)
sofort at once; immediately
sollen to be (supposed) to
soll is/are to; is/are supposed to
der **Sommer** Summer
die **Sonderbestellung** (-en) special order
das **Sortiment** (-e) product range
Spanien Spain
spanisch *adj.* Spanish
später later
der **Speck** bacon
der **Spediteur** (-e) freight forwarder
die **Spedition** (-en) "   "
die **Speisekarte** (-n) menu
  sich spezialisieren auf to specialise
    in

die **Spezialität** (-en) speciality
der **Spielwarenhersteller** (-) toy
    manufacturer
sprechen *str.* to speak
das **Steak** (-s) steak
stimmen to be right
das **stimmt** that's right
stören to bother; disturb
stornieren to cancel (contract)
strapazierfähig hard-wearing
der **Streik** (-s) strike
der **Stricker** (-) knitter
die **Strickwaren** *pl.* knitted goods, knitwear
das **Stück** (-e) piece; item
der **Stückpreis** (-e) price per item
suchen to look for
die **Suppe** (-n) soup

T

der **Tag** (-e) day
der **Tee** tea
das **Teil** (-e) component; (spare) part
die **Telefaxnummer** (-n) fax number
die **Telefonnummer** (-n) telephone
    number
der **Teller** (-) plate
der **Termin** (-e) appointment
teuer expensive
teurer more expensive
der **Tisch** (-e) table
der **Tomatensalat** tomato salad
die **Torte** (-n) gâteau; flan
trinken *str.* to drink
tun *str.* to do
  es tut mir leid I'm sorry
typisch typical

U

über above
übermorgen the day after tomorrow
die **Uhr** hour; o'clock
um around; at (time expressions)
um wieviel Uhr? at what time?
um 10 Uhr at 10 o'clock
umfassen *sep.* to include
der **Umsatz** turnover
und and
ungefähr approximately
uns us; to us
unser (e) our
unter under

unter welcher Nummer? on what number?
das **Unternehmen** (-) company; enterprise
der **Urlaub** (-e) holiday
die **USA** *pl.* the USA

V

verbinden *str.* to connect; put through
vereinbaren to agree on
verheiratet married
der **Verkauf** (Verkäufe) sale
verkaufen to sell
die **Verkaufsabteilung** sales department
der **Verkehr** traffic
verlangen to ask for; demand
vernünftig sensible
die **Verpackung** packaging
verschieden various; different
die **Verspätung** (-en) delay
verstehen *str.* to understand
der **Vertrag** (Verträge) contract
der/die **Vertreter/in** representative
verwenden to use
verzollt duty paid
viel much; many; a lot
vielen Dank many thanks; thank you very much
viel Glück! good luck!
vielleicht perhaps
von from; of
vor before
der **Vormittag** (-e) morning
der **Vorrat** (-räte) stock; supply
auf **Vorrat** in stock
die **Vorspeise** (-n) first course
vorstellen *sep.* to introduce
vorverlegen *sep.* to bring forward
die **Vorwahl** area code

W

wählen to choose
wann? when?
war was
warten to wait
warum? why?
was? what?
was für? what kind of?
der **Wein** (-e) wine

der **Weinkenner** connoisseur of wine
weiß white
der **Weißwein** white wine
welche (r,s)? which?
der **Weltruf** world-wide reputation
wenn if; when; whenever
wer? who?
die **Werbeagentur** (-en) advertising agency
der **Whisky** whisky
wichtig important
wie as; like
wie? how? what?
wie bitte? I beg your pardon? I'm sorry?
wieder again
wiederholen to repeat
auf **Wiederhören** good-bye (used on telephone)
auf **Wiedersehen** good-bye
wieviel(e)? how much? how many?
wieviel Uhr ist es? what time is it?
der **Winter** Winter
die **Winterkollektion** (-en) Winter collection
wir we
wissen *str.* to know (facts)
die **Woche** (-n) week
wohnen to live
wollen to want to
wollen wir ...? shall we ...?
das **Wort** (Wörter) word
das **Wort erteilen** to hand over to
worum? what about?

Z

die **Zahl** (-en) figure; number
die **Zahlung** (-en) payment
die **Zahlungsbedingungen** *pl.* terms of payment
zeigen to show
die **Zeit** (-en) time
zur Zeit at the moment
der/das **Zentimeter** (-) centimetre
das **Zentrum** (Zentren) centre
die **Zigarette** (-n) cigarette
die **Zigarre** (-n) cigar
zu to; too
der **Zucker** sugar
zufrieden happy; pleased; satisfied
zum ersten Mal for the first time
zurück back
zurückrufen *sep. str.* to call back
die **Zusammenarbeit** collaboration

A

to **be able** können
above über
abroad im Ausland
Accounts Department die Rechnungsabteilung
to **be acquainted with** kennen
address die Adresse (-n)
advertising agency die Werbeagentur (-en)
after nach
afternoon der Nachmittag (-e)
again wieder
against gegen
age das Alter
to **agree** (on) vereinbaren
all right! in Ordnung! ist gut!
all together insgesamt
to **allow** erlauben
to **be allowed to** dürfen
already schon
also auch
aluminium das Aluminium
American (citizen) der/die Amerikaner/in
American *adj.* amerikanisch
to **amount to** betragen *str.*
and und
anything else noch etwas
apple juice der Apfelsaft
appointment der Termin (-e)
approximately ungefähr
area die Gegend (-en)
area code die Vorwahl
around um
as als; wie
to **ask** fragen
to **ask for** verlangen
at an; bei (someone's premises); um (time)

B

back zurück
bank account das Konto (Konten)
bank transfer die Banküberweisung (-en)
barrel das Faß (Fässer)

to **be** sein
beauty products die Schönheitsprodukte *pl.*
beer das Bier
before vor
beg: I beg your pardon! Entschuldigung!
better besser
big groß
bill die Rechnung (-en)
both beide
to **bother** stören
bottle die Flasche (-n)
bottled beer das Flaschenbier
boy der Junge (-n)
branch (of company) die Niederlassung (-en)
bread das Brot
briefcase die Aktentasche (-n)
to **bring** bringen
to **bring forward** vorverlegen *sep.*
British britisch
brochure die Broschüre (-n)
builders' merchant der Baumarkt (-märkte)
building company die Baufirma (-firmen)
business die Geschäfte *pl.*
business card die Karte (-n)
business trip die Geschäftsreise (-n)
busy (person) beschäftigt
busy (tel. line) besetzt
but aber
butter die Butter
to **buy** kaufen
by (in dimensions) mal

C

to **call** rufen *str.; tel* anrufen *sep.*
to **call back** zurückrufen *sep.*
to **be called** heißen *str.*
can kann; können
to **cancel** (appointment) absagen *sep.*
to **cancel** (contract) auflösen *sep.*, stornieren
car das Auto (-s)
carriage paid frei Haus
casual salopp
catalogue der Katalog (-e)
centimetre der/das Zentimeter (-)

	centre das Zentrum (Zentren)	
to	**change** ändern	
	cheese der Käse	
	child das Kind (-er)	
	chocolate die Schokolade	
to	**choose** wählen	
	chosen gewählt	
	cigar die Zigarre (-n)	
	cigarette die Zigarette (-n)	
to	**clean** putzen	
	coffee der Kaffee	
	collaboration die Zusammenarbeit	
	colleague der Kollege (-n, -n)/ die Kollegin (-nen)	
	colour die Farbe (-n)	
to	**come** kommen *str.*	
to	**come to** machen	
	what does that come to? was macht das?	
	company das Unternehmen (-)	
	competition die Konkurrenz; der Wettbewerb	
	component das Teil (-e)	
	computer department die EDV-Abteilung	
	conference die Konferenz (-en)	
to	**confirm** bestätigen	
	connoisseur of beer/wine der Bier-/Weinkenner	
to	**connect** verbinden *str.*	
	contract der Vertrag (Verträge)	
	correct richtig	
to	**correspond to** entsprechen *str.*	
to	**cost** kosten	
	could könnte/n	
	country das Land (Länder)	
	crate die Kiste (-n)	
	cuisine die Küche	
	customer der Kunde (-n); die Kundin (-nen)	

D

date das Datum (Daten)
day der Tag (-e)
the day after tomorrow übermorgen
delay die Verspätung (-en)
delivery time die Lieferzeit (-en)
department die Abteilung (-en)
depend: it all depends das kommt darauf an
desk der Schreibtisch (-e)
dessert die Nachspeise (-n)
diameter der Durchmesser (-)

diary der Kalender (-)
different andere(r,s); verschieden
direct (ly) direkt
discount (on quantity) der Rabatt (-e); (for cash/prompt payment) das Skonto (Skonti)
district die Gegend (-en)
to **do** machen
don't mention it bitte schön; nichts zu danken
draught beer Bier vom Faß
to **drink** trinken *str.*
Dutch holländisch *adj.*
duty paid verzollt

E

easy leicht
to **eat** essen *str.*
EC die EG
electronic data processing die EDV
to **employ** beschäftigen
employee der/die Mitarbeiter/in
in employment berufstätig
engaged *(tel.)* besetzt
engineer der/die Ingenieur/in
England England
English (language) das Englisch
enjoy your lunch! Mahlzeit!
enjoy your meal! Guten Appetit!
especially besonders
Europe Europa
European europäisch
everything alles
exact (ly) genau
to **exist** existieren
to **expect** erwarten
expensive teuer
export der Export (-e)
to **export** exportieren
Export Department die Exportabteilung

F

factory die Fabrik (-en)
family firm der Familienbetrieb (-e)
fax number die Telefaxnummer (-n)
Finance Department die Finanzabteilung
fine fein
fine! ist gut!
I'm fine es geht mir gut

firm die Firma (Firmen)
first course die Vorspeise (-n)
fish der Fisch
for für; (time phrases) seit
for example zum Beispiel
France Frankreich
free frei
freight forwarder der Spediteur (-e);
   die Spedition (-en)
fresh frisch
fried gebraten
from von; (a place) aus
full (up) satt

G

gâteau die Torte (-n)
German deutsch *adj.*
German (citizen) der/die Deutsche
German (language) das Deutsch
Germany Deutschland
to **get** bekommen *str.*
to **get in touch with** erreichen
girl das Mädchen (-)
to **give** geben *str.*
glass das Glas
to **go** gehen *str.*
good gut
good-bye auf Wiedersehen; *(tel.)* auf
   Wiederhören
Good luck! Viel Glück!
goods in stock der Lagerartikel (-)
Great Britain Großbritannien
to **guarantee** garantieren

H

half halb *(adj.)*
to **hand over to someone** jemandem das
   Wort erteilen
handbook das Handbuch (-bücher)
hard-wearing strapazierfähig
to **have** haben *str.*
to **have** (to eat/drink) nehmen *str.*
he er
head of department der/die
   Abteilungsleiter/in
headquarters der Hauptsitz (-e)
hello! Guten Morgen/Tag/Abend!;
   Hallo! (informal.)
to **help** helfen *str.*
helpful behilflich
here hier

here you are bitte schön
high hoch
highest höchst
high quality hochwertig
him ihn
holiday der Urlaub (-e)
home: in the home market im Inland
house das Haus (Häuser)
how? wie?
how are you? wie geht es Ihnen?
how much/many? wieviel(e)?

I

ice (-cream) das Eis
if wenn
ill krank
immediately sofort
important wichtig
in in
to **include** umfassen
income das Einkommen
to **increase** steigen *str.*
increased gestiegen
industry die Industrie (-n)
to **inform** Bescheid sagen
to **install** montieren
interesting interessant
international international
into in
to **introduce** vorstellen *sep.*
is/are to soll/en
it (subj.)er; sie; es; (obj.) ihn; sie; es
it's about ...... es geht um ......
Italian italienisch *adj.*
Italy Italien
item das Stück (-e)
item in stock der Lagerartikel (-)

J

journey die Reise (-n)
juice der Saft (Säfte)
jumper der Pullover (-)

K

knitter der/die Stricker/in
knitwear die Strickwaren *pl.*
to **know** (be acquainted with) kennen;
   (know a fact) wissen *str.*

L

ladies and gentlemen! meine
  Herrschaften!
large groß
last letzt
later später
to leave a message etwas ausrichten *sep.*
left; on the left links
let's say ... sagen wir ...
letter der Brief (-e)
  by letter per Brief
like wie
to like mögen
little klein
  a little etwas
to live wohnen
long lang
  for a long time lange
to look for suchen
lot; a lot viel(e)
luck das Glück

M

machine die Maschine (-n)
made of aus
to make machen
main course das Hauptgericht (-e)
man der Herr (-n, -en)
man's sweater der Herrenpullover (-)
Managing Director der/die
  Geschäftsführer/in
to manufacture herstellen *sep.*
manufacturer der Hersteller (-)
many viele
market der Markt (Märkte)
marketing das Marketing
Marketing Department die
  Marketing-Abteilung
marketing manager der/die
  Marketing-Leiter/in
market share der Marktanteil (-e)
married verheiratet
material das Material (-ien)
matter: that doesn't matter das
  macht nichts
may dürfen
me mich
  (to/for) me mir
meal die Mahlzeit (-en)
to mean meinen
measurement das Maß (-e)
meat das Fleisch

medium (steak) halbdurch
medium-sized mittelgroß
meeting die Besprechung (-en); die
  Konferenz (-en)
mention: don't mention it! nichts zu
  danken!
menu die Speisekarte (-n)
middle mittlere (r, s) adj.
milk die Milch
millimetre der/das Millimeter (-)
mineral water das Mineralwasser
minus minus
Miss Frau
misunderstanding das Mißverständnis
  (-se)
model die Ausführung (-en); das
  Modell (-e)
modern modern
moment der Augenblick (-e); der
  Moment (-e)
  at the moment im Augenblick/
  Moment; zur Zeit
month der Monat (-e)
more mehr
morning der Morgen (-); der Vormittag
  (-e)
Mr Herr
Mrs; Ms Frau
much viel
my mein(e)

N

name der Name (-n, -n)
naturally natürlich
new neu
Netherlands die Niederlande *pl.*
next nächst
no nein
no; not a; not any kein(e)
no doubt sicherlich
no, thank you danke
non-smoker der/die Nichtraucher/in
norm die Norm (-en)
not nicht
not at all gar nicht
to note notieren
nothing nichts
now jetzt
number (tel./house no.) die
  Nummer (-n); (figure; digit) die Zahl
  (-en)

O

occasion das Mal (-e)
occasionally ab und zu
o'clock Uhr
at ten o'clock um zehn Uhr
of von
of course natürlich
offer das Angebot (-e)
to offer anbieten *sep.; str.*
office das Büro (-s)
OK! in Ordnung!
old alt
older älter
on auf
one *pron.* man
only nur
or oder
orange juice der Orangensaft
order die Bestellung (-en)
to order bestellen
order number die Bestellnummer (-n)
original (distinctive) originell
other andere(r,s)
our unser(e)

P

packaging die Verpackung
paper plate der Pappteller (-)
part der Teil (-e); (spare part) das Teil (-e)
payment die Zahlung (-en)
per pro
percent das Prozent
perhaps vielleicht
piece das Stück (-e)
preferably lieber
place der Platz (Plätze)
plastic der Kunststoff (-e); das Plastik
plate der Teller (-)
please bitte
to please freuen
pleased to meet you! freut mich!
plus plus
popular beliebt
possible möglich
it's possible es geht
to postpone aufschieben *sep.*
potato chips die Pommes frites *pl.*
pound (sterling; weight) das Pfund
practical praktisch
price der Preis (-e)
price list die Preisliste (-n)

price per item der Stückpreis (-e)
problem das Problem (-e)
to produce produzieren; herstellen *sep.*
product das Produkt (-e)
product range das Sortiment (-e)
production die Produktion
Production Department die Produktionsabteilung
purchase der Einkauf (-käufe)
to purchase kaufen; einkaufen *sep.*
Purchasing Department die Einkaufsabteilung
purchasing manager der/die Einkaufsleiter/in
to put on the bill aufschreiben *sep.; str.*
to put through *(tel.)* verbinden *str.*

Q

quality die Qualität
question die Frage (-n)
quite ganz

R

rather eher
to reach erreichen
to receive bekommen *str.*
reception desk der Empfang
to recommend empfehlen *str.*
red wine der Rotwein
relatively relativ
to remain bleiben *str.*
to repeat wiederholen
representative der/die Vertreter/in
restaurant proprietor der Gastwirt (-e)
right richtig
to be right stimmen
right: on the right rechts
to rise steigen *str.*
risen gestiegen
roast gebraten
round rund *adj.*

S

salad der Salat (-e)
sale der Verkauf (-käufe)
sales department die Verkaufsabteilung

sample das Muster (-)
satisfied zufrieden
to say sagen
schnapps der Schnaps
Scotland Schottland
Scottish schottisch *adj.*
seat der Platz (Plätze)
secretary die Sekretärin (-nen)
to see sehen *str.*
selection of cheeses die Käseauswahl
to sell verkaufen
sensible vernünftig
shade card der Farbstreifen (-)
shall we ...? wollen wir ...?
share (of) der Anteil (an)
she sie
to show zeigen
since (time) seit
single (unmarried) ledig
to sit down Platz nehmen
size die Größe (-n)
small klein
to smoke rauchen
so also
something etwas
something else noch etwas
somewhat etwas
sorry: I'm sorry es tut mir leid
I'm sorry? wie bitte?
soup die Suppe (-n)
Spain Spanien
Spanish spanisch *adj.*
spare part das Ersatzteil (-e)
to speak sprechen *str.*
speciality die Spezialität (-en)
to specialise in sich spezialisieren auf
special order die Sonderbestellung
to spell buchstabieren
standard die Norm (-en)
to stay bleiben *str.*
steak das Steak (-s)
still noch
stock der Vorrat (-räte)
in stock auf Lager
store das Lager (-)
strawberry die Erdbeere (-n)
strike der Streik (-s)
successful erfolgreich
sugar der Zucker
to suit passen
to be suitable for sich eignen für
Summer der Sommer
supplier der Lieferant (-en)
to supply liefern

T

table der Tisch (-e)
to take nehmen *str.*
tall hoch
to taste schmecken
tasted (good) geschmeckt
tea der Tee
telephone line der Anschluß (-schlüsse)
telephone number die Telefonnummer (-n)
to tell erzählen
tell me ... sagen Sie ...
terms of payment die Zahlungsbedingungen *pl.*
terms of supply die Lieferbedingungen *pl.*
than als
to thank danken
thank you danke; vielen Dank
that das
that is; that means das heißt
the der; die; das
then dann
there da; dort
there is/are es gibt
these diese
they sie
thickness of glass die Glasstärke
to think denken; (believe) glauben; (be of the opinion) meinen
this diese(r,s)
this afternoon heute nachmittag
this morning heute vormittag
time die Zeit (-en); (occasion) das Mal(-e)
for the first time zum ersten Mal
what time is it? wieviel Uhr ist es?
times (in dimensions) mal
tired müde
to zu; nach
today heute
tomorrow morgen
tomorrow morning morgen vormittag
too (also) auch; zu
traffic der Verkehr
to try (out) probieren
turnover der Umsatz
type of cheese die Käsesorte (-n)
typical typisch

U

under unter
to **understand** verstehen *str.*
until bis
urgent dringend
us: to/for us uns
USA die USA *pl.*
to **use** verwenden
usually normalerweise

V

various verschieden
very sehr
visit der Besuch (-e)

W

to **wait** warten
waitress! Fräulein!
to **want to** wollen
was war
we wir
week die Woche (-n)
well gut
well done (steak) durchgebraten
well, ... also, ...
were waren
what? was? wie?
what kind of? was für?
when (past time) als; (whenever; future time) wenn

when? wann?
which? welche(r, s)?
whisky der Whisky
white weiß
who? wer?
whole ganz
why? warum?
wide breit
willingly gern(e)
window das Fenster (-)
wine der Wein (-e)
winter der Winter
winter collection die Winterkollektion (-en)
with mit
without ohne
woman die Frau (-en)
woman's sweater der Damenpullover (-)
wood das Holz
word das Wort (Worte/Wörter)
to **work** arbeiten
working (employed) berufstätig
world-wide reputation der Weltruf
would like möchte/n
to **write** schreiben *str.*

Y

year das Jahr (-e)
yes ja
you Sie
(to/for) you Ihnen
your Ihr(e)